Be Still

Elizabeth M. Hoekstra

BETHANY HOUSE PUBLISHERS
MINNEAPOLIS, MINNESOTA 55438

Published by Bethany House Publishers
A Ministry of Bethany Fellowship International
11400 Hampshire Avenue South
Minneapolis, Minnesota 55438
www.bethanyhouse.com

Printed in the United States of America by
Bethany Press International, Minneapolis, Minnesota 55438

ISBN 0–7642–2186–8

To my dear Tea and Testimony sisters in Christ,
for your love, support, and encouragement.

ELIZABETH M. HOEKSTRA is a writer as well as a former RN with a concentration in psychology and maternal health. This is her third book. She and her family make their home in New Hampshire.

Acknowledgments

A self-reflective, deep-digging, spiritually challenging book such as this can only be written when the writer lives securely supported by a number of people. In writing *Be Still*, this security allowed me to be transparent and vulnerable to my reader audience. To highlight just a few:

My thanks and genuine appreciation to Steve Laube, editor extraordinaire, of Bethany House Publishers.

To my mom, Cindy Marriner, for her constant affirmation of my work and this book in particular.

To my patient family: Peter, for nurturing me; Geneva, for teaching me about service; and Jordan, for teaching me about courage. They each reflect what unconditional love means.

My gratitude to my sisters, Mandy Bradford and Melinda Luther, for believing in me, their "little" sister.

My heartfelt thanks to my sister-in-law, Anita Richardson, for precious and much-needed *time*.

Thank you to Integrity Music for permission to use "Name Above All Names."

And my sincerest thanks to my family and all my friends who agreed to have their "stories" told to augment the text of *Be Still*: Mom and Dad Marriner, Mr. and Mrs. T. W. Day, Steve, Margaret, Dottie, Christen, Ruth, Beth, Susan, Heidi, Chris, Melissa, Greg, Michelle, and Betsy.

Contents

Introduction   11

PART ONE: BE STILL
1. Spiritual Attention Deficit Disorder   17
2. Being Human   27
3. Being Spiritual   41
4. Being Quiet   56
5. Being Watchful   72

PART TWO: AND KNOW
6. Wisdom   89
7. Head Knowledge   104
8. Heart Knowledge   121
9. God Knowledge   135

PART THREE: I AM GOD
10. I Am   151
11. God   164
12. Trusting God to Be God   181

Notes   191

Introduction

This book was written in response to my own struggles with guilt, fears, lack of confidence, and letting God take control of my life. In my anxiety, I was so busy trying to stay afloat that I forgot Who was supposed to be the buoyancy in my life. Looking to other sources to keep me afloat only left me further and further adrift. My little craft became heavy with all the burdens I'd accumulated. The more I attempted to balance everything with frenetic activity, the more I deprived myself of what I needed the most—undivided time with the Lord.

Does this sound familiar to you? The problem is that we have grown accustomed to the heightened activity of a frenzied life, and even though we don't like it and recognize we're missing God, there is somehow comfort in its familiarity. We jump from activity to activity, thought to thought, crisis to crisis, with no reprieve, time to think, or even to pray.

But don't you find crisis-dodging exhausting?

If it's so tiring keeping a frantic pace—and we want to stop— why do we keep going, and going, and going? What is the busyness of our lives masking? How can the Lord minister to us, teach us, and be the God of our lives if we aren't paying attention? Perhaps we're afraid of what we'll find in quiet with Him. Maybe we're fearful of silence—and self-revelation—or that different or more spiritual responsibilities will land in our laps if we allow God the time to show us our proper place or places of ministry. When left alone—just God and ourselves—what will we discover? Is ignorance or avoidance of self-introspection bliss? I don't think so. In avoiding quiet time, we deprive ourselves of an essential ingredient to becoming confident in who God designed us to be.

The avenue to this God-given confidence comes from recognizing and eliminating your own spiritual inattentiveness. Confidence will come in being comfortable with how God designed you. It will grow as you embrace more of God's wisdom. It will flourish as you recognize God's personal trustworthiness in your life.

How? The answer lies in a simple but far-reaching, life-changing verse found in Psalms 46:10: "Be still, and know that I am God."

It seems that "Be still, and know that I am God" should require little explanation. Who would think it could take twelve chapters to explain an eight-word verse? At face value it does seem simple, but the magnitude of "be still" has held me hostage in its depth and breadth for much of my adult life. I knew that deep within its folds was the remedy I yearned for to calm my frenetic life. It seemed I couldn't study any other passage of Scripture without questioning how "Be still, and know that I am God" could be applied. I asked, "What changes do I have to make to 'be still'? What don't I 'know' about 'I am God'?" It's taken years not only to understand what "be still" means, but also to attempt to implement a still lifestyle. In a sense, I've barely scratched the surface—I know that God isn't finished with me yet!

"Be still . . ." is at the very core of our belief system as Christians. Being still requires complete surrender to God as the one and only God worthy of our trust—a daunting task! That's why I've endeavored to write such a comprehensive study on what is required to "be still," what it means to "know," and who the Lord is in "I am God."

This is not a book about simplifying your life—though that may well be a by-product of adopting an inner stillness. The stillness I'd like to introduce isn't as much about an actual quiet life as it is about how you respond to busyness. Do you walk through the responsibilities of your life with inner peace, confidence, and conviction? Or do you barrel through with a harried, frazzled, and disorganized approach? This book will help stop the crisis-dodging life that so many people unwittingly have jumped into. This book will help you weed out the extraneous pieces of your life that are snatching time from the Lord. This book is about believing you are capable of quiet and serenity in the midst of the life God has given you, because He is capable of taking care of all the clutter that we tend to accumulate.

Charles Swindoll writes in his book *Intimacy With the Almighty*, "An inner restlessness grows within us when we refuse to get alone and examine our own hearts, including our motives. As our lives begin to pick up the debris that accompanies a lot of activities and involvements, we can train ourselves to go right on, to stay active, to be busy in the Lord's work. Unless we discipline ourselves to pull back, to get alone for the hard work of self-examination in times of solitude, serenity will remain only a distant dream."[1] This "self-examination" is a technique I have explored in this book.

At each chapter end are "Stillness in Action" points to assist you in concentrating on a specific way you can practice stillness. There will also be a suggested memory verse about God's promises concerning stillness, wisdom, and His character.

If you don't already, I strongly suggest that you use a journal on a regular basis to document your times with the Lord. This may be simply an outline of what you're studying in Scripture, personal letters written to the Lord, or a diary—including all the details of your life. Whatever style suits your needs and personality is what's right for you.

I am keenly aware of Bible verses that caution me not to add to or detract from God's Holy Word. Psalms 12:6 and 18:30 declare, "The words of the Lord are flawless," and Proverbs 30:6 says, "Do not add to his words." I remember these as cautionary notes when I start to explain or interpret passages in the Bible. So I submit the following words to the Lord and to you as readers: "May the words of my mouth and the meditation of my heart be pleasing in your sight, O Lord" (Psalm 19:14).

PART ONE

Be Still

CHAPTER ONE

Spiritual Attention Deficit Disorder

"Be still before the Lord
and wait patiently for Him."

PSALM 37:7

I remember when the reality of Attention Deficit Disorder (ADD) struck me—literally—in the face. I was flying from cold New Hampshire, on a packed plane, to warm Florida. Our destination being sun and sea air, spirits were high among my fellow travelers.

Then "Jerrod" happened.

No doubt we have all known or experienced a Jerrod in our lives: about seven years old, missing a front tooth, and so active that even with seat belt restraint, legs and arms jerk and twitch almost constantly.

Once the plane reached cruising altitude, the mother in this case unstrapped Jerrod and turned him loose.

First he ran up and down the aisle several times, slapping the back of each seat as he passed. His mother's half-attempts—"Jerrod!

Jerrod!"—at stopping him only increased his playful mood. When the flight attendants started wheeling the refreshment cart down the aisle, Jerrod's mother corralled him back into his seat—right across the aisle from me. His feet, apparently hot from running, were soon bare, and he started playing catch with a sneaker above his head. As he tossed the shoe increasingly higher, his mother tried to catch it, but he was too quick. In one final attempt to grab it, she clutched the heel, but Jerrod stood up and yanked it away from her. Over-balanced on his feet, the shoe went flying. Out of the corner of my eye I watched it arc sideways, and, before I could react, hit me on the cheek.

Smarting from the impact, and angry at Jerrod's mother, I picked up the sneaker and handed it across the aisle to the tight-lipped, obviously embarrassed woman. She sheepishly mouthed, "Sorry," and grabbed her son by the collar. Sitting him down hard in his seat, and clicking his seat belt in place, I heard her say, "*Now, be still!*"

A flight attendant quickly served him a soft drink and nuts, but even as he ate, his high-pitched, excited voice flitted from topic to topic.

I drank my tea and rubbed my cheek thoughtfully. I looked past the two people to my left and out the window at the God's-eye view of the world below me.

Yes, be still.

"Be still, and know that I am God" (Psalm 46:10).

Be quiet.

Be calm.

Be tranquil.

Be peaceful.

Though Jerrod may or may not have had clinical ADD, I felt the effects of his lack of self-control. Thinking on the verse about being still, I began to wonder just how it came to be that David was inspired to write those words.

Does the Lord look at our frantic lives and seek to control our reckless pace? Does He feel the pain of our misappropriated actions? You bet He does. Does He feel frustrated with the careless use of our time, bodies, and gifts? Like Jerrod's mother, He may well feel like taking us by the collar and saying, "*Now, be still!*"

But the question screams from our whirlwind, breakneck, helter-skelter lives: *HOW?*

How can a mother of four children under the age of ten be still? With jam decorating the walls, dirty toilets from a misguided, potty-training two-year-old boy, and the phone constantly interrupting her attempts at order, how can she find a moment of peace, never mind *stillness?*

Or how about a husband and father who gives his best hours to his job, grabs a drive-thru meal on the way to church for his committee meeting, and then arrives home to a stack of bills waiting to be paid?

Consider also Christians who are confined because of bondage to fear, physical ailments, addictions, control, or abuse. Striking out against these kinds of imprisonment, constantly trying to grab hold of the security of God, they are in perpetual evasive motion.

Where is stillness for any of these people? Stillness of spirit, quietness of action, peaceful lives. Indeed, is stillness even available to them, or to you?

Again, the answer lies buried in Psalm 46:10. This gem, "Be still, and know that I am God," is a treasure small in countenance, easy to overlook, yet powerful. There isn't a verse that more succinctly sums up the relationship that God desires we have with Him. He wants us to allow Him to be God, to act and work as only He can. He wants us to sit on our uselessly fluttering hands and let His strong hands do the work.

Look at the rest of that verse: "I will be exalted among the nations, I will be exalted in the earth." Can you sense His frustration? He sounds impatient; in effect, saying, "Be quiet, people, I am *God.* There is nothing you can do but let me be God. In my almighty power, only I will be praised, only I can be God of the earth. So stop fretting, and let me do my job!"

But how can we stop fretting when there is so much to worry about, so many responsibilities, so many worthy things that require our attention? We can't just stop everything!

Of course not. Being still in God's eyes isn't shirking the responsibilities and obligations He has entrusted to us. He has given us personal gifts, family, ministry, perhaps a profession, and He wants us to give our wholehearted efforts to those.

But far too many Christians suffer from what I call spiritual attention deficit disorder. We move through life reacting impulsively to influences around us. Our hyperactive pace leaves little room for reflection and inner quiet. Our attention spans are too short to spend serious time in prayer—the "to do" checklist stubbornly scrolls through our minds. Spiritual ADD interrupts a close walk with the Lord and ultimately inhibits spiritual quiet.

If you have ever spent time with a truly hyperactive child who has the attention span of a tornado, you know firsthand the strong desire for stillness. Such an experience leaves you feeling emotionally and physically spent. A hyperactive, attention deficit person cannot assimilate too much information. His or her brain goes on overload and starts to misfire, reacting impulsively to various stimuli. Incomplete thoughts and actions typify an ADD person, who may use dangling sentences, fail to complete tasks, and suffer from general disorganization. It's not that he doesn't want to be more focused, but rather that his whirling brain won't allow him to be.

ATTENTION–GRABBERS

The same can be true in our spiritual lives. A misfiring spirituality produces inattentiveness to God's voice. When we are unfocused, the Lord sometimes has to use unpleasant means to grab our attention.

A friend of mine, who had been married for five years, was dealing with the devastation of infertility. Employed at a preschool, daily interaction with children increased her disappointment and her anger at God for what she felt was His denial of her deepest desire. She rejected her husband's offer of emotional support, she withdrew from friends, and she stopped attending Christian functions.

Her depression fueled her need to stay busy. In an attempt to get away from the pain of infertility, she scheduled her days down to the minute: ten minutes for breakfast, eight hours for work, thirty minutes for cleaning and laundry, one hour at the gym. She even scheduled exactly eight hours of sleep. What she neglected to schedule, intentionally or subconsciously, was time with the Lord. She felt that if she controlled the sweep of time, nothing more could hurt her. If she avoided God, she would avoid disappointment in how He functioned.

What she didn't know was that He desperately wanted to get her attention. He wanted to comfort her in her pain and offer her hope. And because her name was written in the Book of Life, He wasn't going to let her slide. Her soul meant too much to Him.

First, the Holy Spirit convicted her conscience, and she started to feel a bit guilty. Her friends called to comfort her, but she brushed them off, saying she was too busy. Internally, she quieted the niggling by adding more activities to her schedule.

It was as if the Lord knew gentleness wasn't going to work there. Something harder, firmer, was needed to get her attention.

Like a concrete wall.

As if symbolically, her controlled, measured life literally spun out of control driving home from the gym one evening. She doesn't remember the accident—or hitting the wall—only that she woke up with blood dripping from a gash in her head. Shards of glass had pierced her skull and imbedded in her brain, and she underwent several hours of surgery. The doctor told her a few inches one way, and the glass would have seriously impaired her speech; a fraction of an inch another way, and she would have been killed.

A pretty serious wake-up call, wouldn't you say? The accident served its purpose. Please understand, I'm not saying God *made* the accident happen. But I believe He allowed it to happen. There's a big difference. Knowing He could have miraculously stopped her car and didn't for her own good is the distinction. She promptly went to her knees, recognizing how far she had drifted from the Lord. She saw that He could have called her home at the concrete wall, and she knew that she would have had to answer for her independent steps away from Him. He got her attention; she repented.

What has He done in your life to get you back on track? Illness? A guilty conscience? Near-misses? Strained relationships?

In the past when I have started to drift off, thinking I could conquer the sea of life on my own, the Lord has always restored my steering by showing me how fragile my little craft is. (Pardon this analogy—my maiden name is Marriner.) I'd start to feel tired and discouraged. Irritation became my sail, billowing out from me at the slightest infraction of others. Suddenly, the Lord would allow a squall—a bout of depression, an illness, insomnia—to really rock my boat; and then, reeling about in its wake, I'd cry out to Him, realizing I had gone off course. He always welcomed me back into His fleet, and I gratefully fell into place behind His flagship. He'd gotten my attention again. All I needed to remember was to stay focused on Him in the first place.

This spiritual focus doesn't come easy. We spend a lot of time in motion, but is it the right kind of motion?

"DOING" FOR GOD

We "do" so much in the name of the Lord—ministry, service, volunteer work—that we sometimes forget who we are doing it for. We act as if the Lord has a giant checklist in heaven, crossing off accomplishments as we perform them. But who "assigned" this list? Us, or the Lord? If you suffer from spiritual ADD, the lines are blurred not only about who you are serving but why, where, and how. Imagine how our gracious heavenly Father feels when we scurry and flutter about Him. I can see Him reaching out His steady, powerful hand to engulf our bobbing heads: "Be still, child, be still."

ACTIVE STILLNESS

Being still actually requires action, because being still is a mindset, a way of being: simply, a lifestyle. Being still requires you to embrace yourself and your limitations. It's an internal steadiness, a peacefulness, a calm spirit. Being still in the Lord is like having a personal internal compass constantly realigning your body, soul, and mind heavenward.

As your personal compass stays straight-arrowed to Christ, you become free of the gravitational pull of "proven" Christianity, i.e., all the activities you undertake to demonstrate your faith: workshops, conferences, training courses, and Bible studies. Do these in and of themselves make you become still before God? Not likely. They may help you reorganize your life, clarify your priorities, and give you the tools to become more peaceful, but the inner stillness you desire does not come through busyness for the kingdom.

Being still is not only desiring stillness but being comfortable with solitude—being content with your inner and outer self. It is being confident in the skills God has given you and using them quietly. Being still is about being comfortable with who you are and not being apologetic for who you aren't.

Do you long for this internal tranquillity? Do you want a still spirit amid the chaos of your life? The good news is that this stillness is available to you—to every Christian who wants it.

WHERE ARE WE GOING?

Did you know that the verb "to be" is the most frequently used verb in the English language? It is one of the few passive verbs, implying no movement or action.

Learning to be still requires a process—a sequence of events that teach you and equip you to be able to be still in the Lord.

Part of the process is simply being quiet and waiting on the Lord. Part of learning to be still is understanding the wisdom that comes from heaven. Part of relinquishing our stillness to the Lord is to first understand who God is.

And that is what we will discover in the next few pages. The stillness you desire in your spirit, down in the depths of your very being, is the same desire God has for you. He doesn't want us to live chaotic, hyperactive, attention deficit lives. He doesn't want us to be so burned-out that we tune out our own spiritual and physical needs, never mind those of our families.

I believe He wants us to be confident enough in our spiritual selves to be able to ignore the extraneous matters that are vying for our attention. He wants us to "put it all in perspective," allowing Him to be the peace-keeper. He wants us to be free from what I call "spirituality bondage"—a need to prove our spiritualness.

We can't be still in or by our own actions. We can't plaster it on our souls like a Band-Aid and hope it sticks when we swim through turbulent waters. No, stillness of spirit can only come from God.

IT DOES HAPPEN!

I have a friend, in her seventies now, who persevered through many hardships before coming face-to-face with the Lord and even now continues to struggle with personal difficulties. She has come to understand the meaning of "Be still, and know that I am God."

As a young woman in her twenties, she met and fell in love with a handsome man. Two days after they married, her husband was struck by a speeding car while crossing the street. He died, leaving her lonely and confused. Drink became her soul mate. A second marriage, a few years later, lasted for nineteen years despite constant verbal and physical abuse. She longed for a child but never conceived. Again she found solace in the bottle. Her bruised body and degenerative arthritis held her hostage to constant pain that even alcohol couldn't erase. After her second divorce, in an era when abuse and divorce were never spoken of, she started attending Alcoholics Anonymous (AA) meetings. Her desire for drink had gone beyond her control, and a physician finally said to her, "This is a fatal illness for which there is no cure."

Knowing she was physically and emotionally addicted, and headed for certain death if she continued drinking, she cried out to the Lord for a miracle: "I'll turn things over to You. You take it until I'm ready to take it back—but it's Yours now."

She's been sober for thirty-four years. And even though the Lord did miraculously take away her obsessive-compulsive habit, her life was not charmed. She married a third time and enjoyed a happy marriage, but, sadly, her husband died of cancer.

Now she lives with a degenerative eye disease that is slowly destroying her eyesight. When I asked her how she coped, what her secret was, she said simply, "Let God take it." So convinced is she of this simple yet profound statement, it's emblazoned on her license plate: LET GOD.

Just let God be God. Let Him do the work. Let Him carry the heavy burdens of your hurts, your jumbled, confusing life, your unnecessary guilt, and your need to succeed.

As you read these pages, I urge you to ask God to speak to you. Drop your frets, your "to do" list, and your self-imposed expectations. Once your hands and arms are free of these heavy burdens, pick up God's cloak of stillness. Imagine wrapping this cloak around you until you feel His warmth and comfort within your heart.

Now sit in a soft, comfortable chair . . . and be still.

Stillness in Action

Think about the areas of your life in which you may be experiencing spiritual attention deficit disorder. Write down times in the past when the Lord has had to turn your world upside down to get your attention, and what the ramifications were of those experiences. Pray for discernment to find out the areas in which He may be speaking to you now.

MEMORY VERSE

"The Lord will fulfill his purpose for me; your love, O Lord, endures forever."

PSALM 138:8

CHAPTER TWO

Being Human

"For you created my inmost being;
you knit me together in my mother's womb.
I praise you because I am fearfully
and wonderfully made."

PSALM 139:13–14

I sat in the front row of a large auditorium. Behind me I could hear three hundred bodies shifting in their seats; I could feel the warm air of their breath on the back of my neck. Though the speaker on the platform was worthy of my attention, my focus was turned inward to my flopping stomach, pounding heart, and tight chest.

Surely I was having a heart attack!

Oh, yes, please let it be a heart attack, so I can have an excuse not to stand in front of this crowd and talk to them! I thought silently.

I glanced at my watch for the tenth time in as many minutes. I had enough time to dash to the bathroom once more before it was my turn to speak. In front of the bathroom mirror, I checked my lipstick, blew my nose, patted my hair. On the outside I looked fine, pulled together, in perfect control. On the inside . . .

"Oh, God," I whispered. "I can't do this. I don't know how to do this!"

In my spirit I heard His response, *Be still, my child. Be still.*

Back in the auditorium, I was called to the front. I tremulously walked toward the stage. My legs felt heavy, as if I couldn't lift them high enough to climb the steps. I was convinced I would trip and fall (*Can they see me shaking?*). When I reached the podium and placed my sweat-stained notes on the stand, I thought if I opened my mouth I'd surely drool.

I looked out over the expectant audience waiting for me to impart words of wisdom, words of encouragement. But all I could do was think back fifteen years to the last time I had been in the same room: when I was a teenager.

It was my high school year-end banquet. I was a sophomore. That school year had been a difficult one. Though my grades were okay, my teachers had hounded me, and eventually punished me, for not speaking out in class. When called upon to answer questions, I always panicked: my throat tightened, and the only way I could respond was to shake my head and make a grunting sound. Even if I knew the answer, I *couldn't* open my mouth to speak. I was sure if I did I would either vomit, garble my speech, or scream. The school year seemed an eternity as they tried every avenue to entice me to speak, but nothing worked. When the banquet arrived, signifying the end of the school year, my relief was profound, knowing I would be attending a different school in the fall. I hoped this would give me a chance to start over.

Never in a million years would I have thought those fifteen years ago that I would be standing in the same room in front of a crowd to speak about the pro-life organization for which I worked.

I gazed out across the room, recognizing only a handful of people, and stammered, "I stood in this same room fifteen years ago, and never dreamed I would be capable of standing in front of a crowd of three hundred to speak. I never thought I would have the courage to speak publicly, but do you know what? *God has healed me!*" I saw faces smile, heads nod, and heard people clap. Then an amazing thing happened. I *was* healed. My hands stopped shaking, my heart settled to a normal rhythm, I stopped gasping for air, and my voice was steady and sure as I gave my prepared speech. I then introduced the next speaker and calmly stepped off the stage. As I sat down next to my boss, he said, "Good job." I smiled and pointed my finger heavenward.

At the end of the evening everyone stood to sing "Amazing Grace" by John Newton. The second stanza brought tears streaming down my face:

'Twas grace that taught my heart to fear,
and grace my fears relieved;
How precious did that grace appear
the hour I first believed!

I have stood and spoken before other crowds, and though I still experience some trepidation, I have never had another panic attack associated with public speaking. God indeed healed me that day, and I believe the reason is in His Word: "Be still, and know that I am God." He didn't expect me to speak on my own, nor did He want me to. He wanted me to need His help. He wanted me to cry out to Him. And when I did call to Him and acknowledge Him, He calmed my spirit and gave me peace.

In my limited humanness, I don't think I could have overcome my terror of public speaking. And I know I'm not the only person to suffer such fright; public speaking is actually one of the most frequently cited personal fears. The core reason is usually the fear of humiliation. What if I spit all over the people in the front row? What if I lose my place and forget what to say? What if I stammer and mix up my words, sounding like a fool? What if I urgently have to go to the bathroom? *What if they realize I'm just a phony?*

Praise God that where our humanness thwarts our progress, His grace begins! Like me, all you have to do is acknowledge Him and ask. Whatever your personal conflicts are, He is there to grab the rope of your humanity on which you have such a tenuous grip.

You don't have to hold on by yourself with your spiritual and emotional muscles screaming for a rest. The Lord's whisper of stillness to me during those panicked minutes comforted me, quieted me, gave me peace, and ultimately provided me with the confidence and strength I needed.

Yes, be still, child. Be still in who you are and in who I created you to be: a human being.

We are first and foremost *beings.* Human beings, spiritual beings, emotional beings. We can't learn how to be still if we don't first understand how we are as humans: how we were created, how we function as beings, and how our finiteness affects our perception of God's infiniteness.

OUR HUMANITY

It is because of our humanity that we need God. It is because of our limitations and the very nature of being human that we need the Lord's cradling hands in our lives.

Human beings are restricted by so many things. Our finite minds, our fragile bodies, our fragmented lives. Even gravity holds us captive. Some restrictions are self-imposed, like personal convictions; others are societal, like obeying the laws of man. These restrictions aren't bad, of course. Personal, environmental, and governmental restrictions are for our protection. But the more these confines darken our free thought, the more we recognize that we need the Lord to illuminate the path that leads to the Truth. It is only because of our human limits that we even recognize our need for Him.

David recognized and wondered at his humanity in Psalm 8:

When I consider your heavens,

the work of your fingers,
the moon and the stars,
which you have set in place,
what is man that you are mindful of him,
the son of man that you care for him?
You made him a little lower than
the heavenly beings
and crowned him with glory and honor.
You made him ruler over the works of your hands;
you put everything under his feet. (italics mine)

Can't you just hear David's awe at our position on earth? With all that God did and can create, the beauty of the sky and earth, the diversity of it all, yet He ordained man to rule over it. It is a tad humbling, don't you think? David was humbled as he recognized his finiteness. He saw just how *small* and insignificant we are compared to God.

Yet God created us to have fellowship and communion with Him. When He created man, He desired a deeper connection between the living creatures He had created and heaven. He wanted intelligent and articulate life to connect, through their *being*, with Him as God.

Enter man and woman.

Apart from Christ himself, Adam and Eve were the closest human beings to God the Father than any other has been or ever will be. Do you ever feel just a little annoyed at them for spoiling Eden for the rest of us? Imagine if they had never partaken of the fruit of knowledge? We would be living in a perfect world, free from sin, guilt, and punishment. Indeed, we would be sitting quietly in the presence of the Lord daily because there would be no need for us to toil!

Despite the original sin, and how much it obviously grieved God, He still kept His promise to mankind and allows us to rule over the earth and all its treasures. Though, regrettably, we don't always do it in a fashion that pleases Him, He graciously keeps giving abundantly to us.

We don't deserve God's compassion, grace, or patience as we fumble our way across His creation. Yet He has allowed us, even given us, the knowledge to better ourselves and our lives. Take the medical field, for example. It is almost as if He is up in heaven doling out small fragments of knowledge about our beings to physicians, scientists, and researchers. But I'm grateful that God hasn't dumped all the answers into medical science's lap. Yes, I certainly hope and pray that cures and vaccines are developed for fatal diseases like cancer or AIDS, but our limited knowledge in the intricate workings of the human body keeps us humbly human. If we had all the answers, it would usurp our need to trust in God's perfect creation of our bodies.

OUR PHYSICAL BODIES

Psalm 139:13–16 gives us a profound look at just how much care God put into creating our physical bodies:

> For you created my inmost being; you knit me together in my mother's womb. I praise you because I am fearfully and wonderfully made; your works are wonderful, I know that full well. My frame was not hidden from you when I was made in the secret place. When I was woven together in the depths of the earth, your eyes saw my unformed body. All the days ordained for me were written in your book before one of them came to be.

We are "fearfully and wonderfully" made. Respectfully and amazingly. Tremulously and remarkably. Shyly and awesomely.

It's hard to imagine an all-powerful God quietly and delicately knitting and weaving us together. But His direct, intimate involvement in forming us is what makes us individuals. Genesis 1:27 says, "So God created man in his own image, in the image of God he created him; male and female he created them." Each of us is created "in the image of God." This is why Psalm 139:14 says we are to praise Him for how we are created, because we are created *like Him*. There is a portion of God's personal characteristics in each of us. And He has so many characteristics and qualities, He has yet to run out of combinations.

In a book I wrote with M. Beth Cutaiar, titled *Just for Girls*, we wrote about girls' developing bodies and how God is intimately involved in each individual's development. This is an excerpt:

> Imagine God standing before a huge canvas. He has a palette in one hand with a giant paintbrush in the other. As he prepares to paint His picture, He mixes a few colors together on His palette to create a new hue He has never used before. He tilts His head, deciding if it is just right. Yes, it is. With broad, firm strokes He covers the canvas with one color. Then He adds smaller splotches of colors. He adds definition with the new colors He's never used before. It takes Him a long time to create this piece so it is distinctly different from others yet has similarities to past paintings. When it is finally done, He is very much pleased. He puts His thumbprint in the upper left corner. There, it is marked with His signature as His creation. And it is perfect in His sight.
>
> So it is with you. You were created perfect in His sight, by Him and for Him. His thumbprint is upon your heart as a seal of ownership of your spirit and soul.[1]

This ownership we talked about is found in 2 Corinthians 1:21–22: "He anointed us, set his seal of ownership on us, and put his Spirit in our hearts as a deposit, guaranteeing what is to come." And then, 2 Corinthians 3:18: "And we, who with unveiled faces all reflect the Lord's glory, are being transformed into his likeness with ever-increasing glory."

He created our bodies, He owns our bodies, He has His plans

for our bodies all mapped out. He also is perfecting our inner beings, "guaranteeing" our future in Him as we are "transformed into his likeness." I'm so glad He promises I will be changed into a resemblance of Him. That's something worth looking forward to!

Our earthly bodies cause us so much distress sometimes. We think we're too fat, too short, too tall, not smart enough, etc. American consumers spend millions of dollars every year on dieting and fitness. That's not to say we shouldn't pursue avenues that keep us healthy, but sometimes we try to alter the very core of how God made our individual bodies. We need to be reminded that we were created just as God wanted us to be: buck teeth, red hair, six-foot-two, farsighted, or whatever your personal physical traits are, because that is the way He could best be glorified through you.

Shyness and insecurity about our bodies is not how God originally designed us. As a matter of fact, in Genesis 2:25 God makes a point of telling us that Adam and Eve weren't bashful about their bodies, saying, "The man and his wife were both naked, and they felt no shame."

Adam and Eve developed shame only after they sinned against the Lord. Their nakedness, which I believe to be both a literal nudity and a figurative recognition of spiritual unworthiness, became obvious to them and they were deeply ashamed. They realized they needed to cover themselves, to hide their nakedness. Yet, interestingly, it was God himself who covered them, as it reads in Genesis 3:21: "The Lord God made garments of skin for Adam and his wife and clothed them." Do you know why God designed the garments for them? Because Adam and Eve didn't know how to do it for themselves—He had not instilled in them an innate knowledge of sewing. He had given them many skills, but garment-making wasn't one of them because they hadn't had a prior need to make clothing. God had to do it for them because He wanted to continue to protect and provide for them.

In essence, when God clothed Adam and Eve, He was stripping

them of any vestiges of stubborn independence. In a most primary way He demonstrated to them their dependence on Him for *everything*. Clothing, food, and protection. And that is where we still are today.

But we have made things worse.

As mankind has drifted further and further from the ideal world of Eden, we've become self-absorbed. Our frantic pace sends us scurrying like squirrels gathering nuts. Sequestered in our subdivisions, church bodies, and work communities, we've lost sight of God's original plan of quiet communion with Him.

It's as if we're looking through the viewfinder of a video camera, only taking sight of what is before us in our own little world. Then we fast forward through our lives, neglecting or ignoring the bigger picture around us.

WHY IN SUCH A HURRY?

Indeed, why are we moving at fast forward? What is so important that it usurps our attention from God himself? Is it the "keeping up with the Joneses" phenomenon? Is it a personal conviction to do better, spend more, buy bigger, have many? Is it a status quo attitude that says, "If you can't beat 'em, join 'em"? Maybe it's simply passivity that sweeps us along with the rest of the pack.

Regardless of the reasons why we all suffer from a spiritual attention deficit disorder, we have found ourselves running to keep up with the pack. I suspect we're looking wistfully behind, hoping God is keeping up with us. But we can't have a connection with God if we're moving too fast to be still.

It is as if there is an invisible wire running straight from God the Father into our very heart-souls. Through this wire, He communicates to us in His language of patience, love, forgiveness, and tenderness. But when we start to pull too hard on the wire, or jump around too much, or confuse it with someone else's wire, we end up in a tangled mess. And what about when it gets kinked and corroded with sin? Messages from God can't complete their journey to our hearts. Whatever the obstacles that stop His words from reaching their destination, He requires us to wait and *be still* while He untangles the mess we have gotten ourselves into.

Imagine if we were to never even get tangled in the first place. Wouldn't our lives run more smoothly, wouldn't we be able to hear God more quickly and more precisely if we avoided the tangles of a complicated life?

THE ART OF STILLNESS

Every summer our family rents a cottage for a week on a pristine lake in mid-New Hampshire. The first summer we did this, Peter, the children, and I excitedly anticipated a week of swimming, boating, sunning, and just being together. When we arrived, I symbolically removed my watch and stuck it in my bag—*now* I was on vacation.

Our daughter, Geneva, who was seven that summer, is the kind of person who needs to know "the plan." She is a self-possessed, structured young woman who thrives in settings of predictability, but who feels fragmented and out of sorts without a plan. She is not a go-with-the-flow kind of individual.

The first two days of vacation she could not relax. She would ask, as soon as we rolled out of bed, what, when, and where the plan was for that day. Not that she wanted constant activity, she just needed a plan to focus on.

It drove me nuts—the whole concept of "vacation" was lost on her.

After many frustrated "I don't knows" from me, she finally realized and became comfortable with the idea that vacation meant *just being*. It meant not having a game plan: it meant swimming for an hour, then sleeping for two; showering at two in the afternoon; eating supper at nine, reading until midnight; eating when you're hungry, sleeping when you're tired.

Geneva had to learn how to be quiet in spirit and not feel frantic in the calmness. I learned a lot watching my child struggle to find her place of restfulness. She grappled with feeling out of control; she needed and wanted to manage our time. But as she released control of what I called her "fear of free time," she found she liked the freedom of no time constraints. She learned how to enjoy our vacation unencumbered by a ticking clock.

Being still in our faith and life is a lost art. Why did I choose the word "art"? Because to me being still implies a gracefulness, a fluidity of faith that permeates the whole being. I visualize stillness as a ballet dancer gliding effortlessly across a misted meadow, arms outstretched as if welcoming the hills, grass, filtered sun, trees, nature itself, to her bosom. She noiselessly flits across the ground, the mist swirling in and out of her skirt hem. She gently twirls over the grass but never breaks a stem. Her dance is directed heavenward; it's not for herself or man's glory, but is a dance of being still in God's creation. The dancer is a part of the peaceful meadow, her solitude a part of the stillness.

So this stillness is an art, a skill, that can become so much a part of your being and your every movement that it's as recognizable as your blue eyes or your brown hair. Unfortunately, our understanding of this kind of fluid stillness is limited by our perception of the world around us. Let me explain.

LIVING WITH BLINDERS

My horse, Galilee, was born in my barn and raised by my hands. By the time he was two years old, he was a gangly, somewhat clumsy, thousand-pound animal; a size and strength I didn't enjoy arguing with. I decided Galilee needed to do something constructive with his life, so I sent him to a trainer who would teach Galilee to pull a cart.

Part of the harness paraphernalia included blinders on the bridle that covered the sides of Galilee's eyes. Humor me for a moment as

I detail the anatomy of a horse. Horses' eyes, located on the sides of their heads, can rotate to give them a nearly 360-degree view around them. Actually, the only place they can't see well is right at the end of their noses. In the wild, horses use a combination of their 360-degree visual field and their acute hearing to be on the alert for predators. To take away a portion of their eyesight or hearing limits their flight instinct.

When I saw Galilee with blinders, I asked his trainer about the effectiveness of blocking a horse's sight when he is driving a cart. Did it make him panic or give him security? He said the blinders help the horse to concentrate on what is ahead of him instead of what is beside or behind him, which could potentially cause him to spook. The blinders compel the horse to be focused on the work at hand, moving forward, pulling the cart behind him. Blinders block out the scary peripheral, giving the horse a view of only what is in front of him. Some racehorses run with blinders, too. Hot-blooded thoroughbreds are sensitive to every distraction, and the blinders force them to focus on the track ahead. If they can't see what is behind them or beside them, they aren't afraid of it. So the blinders act as a form of security.

I learned that part of training a horse to pull a cart is teaching him to trust the driver. If the driver says it's okay with his steady hands and voice to cross a noisy bridge, the horse learns to not only accept the command of moving forward, but he learns to trust that the driver will keep him safe. He has, in effect, relinquished his flight instinct to the calm, quiet hands of the driver holding the reins.

Galilee learned to trust me in the cart behind him. Even though he couldn't see me, he could feel my hands through the reins and hear my encouraging voice. The time came when I needed to start riding him. I felt dubious; riding bridles don't have blinders. Both Galilee and I had grown accustomed to the security of the blinders on his harness. Wouldn't he be frightened by the new sights suddenly visible around him? But I realized I had to trust that he had learned to trust me.

He's eleven now, and I ride him up to five days a week, but I haven't driven him in five years. I can't say we've had an easy time on all of our rides; he does have an active imagination about noises around him. But I can say that when we stopped using the blinders, my confidence in myself and in him actually increased. Why? Because I learned that trusting him not to hurt me equaled his trust in me not to let harm come to him when he wore the blinders.

Does this sound at all familiar to your Christian walk? We, too, are like young horses who want the security of blinders in our Christian faith. Sometimes we don't want to know what horrors are in the periphery of our world. But we get too accustomed to the security of the blinders. We become too comfortable with our blocked vision.

REMOVING THE BLINDERS

Even with the Lord's grace, we still have human blinders attached to our spiritual vision. We are limited by the knowledge of our past on our journey with the Lord, and resolutely focused on what lies straight ahead of us. But God works in the periphery. I think many times we don't even realize how much God is doing for us on the sidelines. I believe God wants us to remove those spiritual blinders so we can see the bigger picture.

In removing the blinders, a whole new world emerges. Granted, it is somewhat scary, even overwhelming. But if we remain quiet under the Lord's directive hands, trusting Him to let no harm come to us, a strange thing happens. We like our newfound freedom of vision. We have a clearer understanding of the world around us. We develop a tolerance for new images and thoughts. Not that we compromise our beliefs or faith, but we suddenly can see the landscape in all its grit or beauty, and we stop fretting about what it is or isn't.

And once we stop fretting about the perceived "what ifs," "what abouts," and "whys," then we find ourselves with just one thought and truth: God has the reins. He has removed our blinders, let us see the world in its entirety, and is still in control! Still guiding us, protecting us, and quieting us under His knowledgeable hands.

We have learned to be steady and still under His trustworthy, strong guidance.

We have learned to just be.

Stillness in Action

Try to identify in what areas of your life you would like to pursue being still. Your job? Your patience with your children? Your relationship with your in-laws? In your journal or prayer book, write out three areas in which you want to work on a still spirit. Start small, by praying for the Lord to give you glimpses of stillness amid chaotic situations.

MEMORY VERSE

"Now the Lord is the Spirit, and where the Spirit of the Lord is, there is freedom. And we, who with unveiled faces all reflect the Lord's glory, are being transformed into his likeness with ever-increasing glory, which comes from the Lord, who is the Spirit."

2 CORINTHIANS 3:17–18

CHAPTER THREE

Being Spiritual

"From birth I was cast upon you;
from my mother's womb
you have been my God."

PSALM 22:10

The phone rang at 6:40 on a cold, dark February morning. You know the feeling you get when the phone rings at that hour— nobody calls before 8:00 A.M, unless there's a crisis.

Sure enough, my grandfather had passed away in the night. He was eighty-eight but had still lived at home with my grandmother in the house they had shared for over fifty years. Though he died peacefully in his sleep, his death was entirely unexpected and sent deep waves of grief over our family. He would be greatly missed.

Before his retirement, my grandfather had been a French teacher, so when my oldest sister was born, he wanted her to call him *Grand-père*, French for Grandfather. In her newfound voice, all she could muster was "Pompere." The name stuck through the rest of his five grandchildren and four great-grandchildren.

Jordan, our active but reserved youngest son, wasn't even a year old when Pompere died. Jordan had last seen my grandfather on Christmas Eve, almost two months prior, during our annual Christmas party at Sweetwood, my grandparents' farm. Pompere loved his four great-grandchildren, and they knew that, but Jordan had actually spent very little time at their home in the course of his short life.

The immediate family gathered at Sweetwood before Pompere's memorial service at the local community church. The subdued atmosphere of the small gathering found Jordan clinging to my neck. We sat quietly in the living room, forming a semi-circle around my grandmother. She sat in her usual big, soft, green chair, but she looked so pale, so tired, so fragile that it seemed the chair would envelop her entirely. In the quietness, Jordan suddenly slid off my lap, toddled over to his great-grandmother, and clambered up onto her lap. He snuggled his head against her shoulder, put one small hand behind her neck, and grabbed her fingers with his other hand.

I felt stunned. Jordan hardly knew his great-grandmother. He had shied away from her attempts at holding him in the past; he was always too busy or in too much of a hurry to be bothered with a hug. But on this day, when my grandmother had such a deep need for love, hugs, kindness, and compassion, Jordan was moved in his wee spirit to minister to her. I believe the Holy Spirit in Jordan, for which his father and I had prayed even prior to his birth, nudged him to reach out to my grandmother. No other human touch would have meant as much to her that day. Because it was ministered by a child, so innocent and pure and obviously straight from the Lord himself, she received comfort in her nearly impossible grief. It was as if He personally reached out to comfort my grandmother, saying, "I am with you still."

She has said to me in retrospect that when Jordan climbed onto her lap, she immediately thought of the words of Job: "The Lord giveth and the Lord taketh away, blessed be the name of the Lord." She knew she would grieve over the loss of Pompere for the remainder of her days, but she also knew that life goes on, and a small piece of Pompere was right there cuddled up on her lap.

I am still in awe, over five years later, of how the Lord could use such a small child to minister in such a big way. But knowing God and His nature, I shouldn't be surprised. The shepherd David was quite young when he began his service to the Lord; Josiah became king of Jerusalem when he was only eight; and John the Baptist jumped for joy in Elizabeth's womb when he "heard" of Jesus' conception. The evidence is that young, even unborn, children have spirits capable of being used for God's glory.

Why is this important to understand? Because we tend to view our spiritual walk as a very adult venture. It is not.

LIKE THE LITTLE CHILDREN

As we noted in chapter 2, God has known us from preconception. He has had a plan for us long before we knew of a need for a plan in our lives. If He is the God of our physical humanness, then He is the God of our spiritual humanness. And that spirituality starts before we are even born.

Look again at Psalm 22:9–10: "Yet you brought me out of the womb; you made me trust in you even at my mother's breast. From birth I was cast upon you; from my mother's womb you have been my God." The Spirit of the living God starts in the quietness of two living cells meeting, cojoining, then dividing, and finally multiplying at a rapid pace. A new human being with a soul has been created.

I am frequently struck with awe at the innocence of my children when I pray over them before I go to bed. Earlier in the evening I've prayed out loud with them, sung to them, given them drinks of water, and snuggled the blankets around them. But after they are asleep, I go back into each of their rooms and rearrange blankets to cover toes, touch foreheads to make sure no one is feverish, and pray one last blessing over them. As I watch their little chests rise and fall in the rhythm of sleep, I am continually humbled by what a privilege it is to have children, these pure gifts from God.

Have you ever watched a child sleep? Their pure abandon is revealed in open palms, flickering eyelids, relaxed, parted lips, serene faces, limp muscles, and steady, deep breathing. They are secure. In the tranquillity of their sleep it is as if we are seeing the stillness of God himself.

In Mark 10:15, it says we are to receive the kingdom of God like children: "I tell you the truth, anyone who will not receive the kingdom of God like a little child will never enter it." We are to receive it unabashedly, innocently, wholeheartedly, with complete trust.

Why is it so hard for us to set aside our adulthood and become like children when it comes to our complete trust in God? Because we are so busy being grown up. Too proud, too self-confident. After all, our bodies are mature; why do we need to become like little children again? I think Paul was trying to illustrate that our adult bodies can't deceive or disguise our inner spiritual growth. We may be grown up in body, but our spiritual growth is much slower.

Just as our bodily development is a growing process, first *in utero*, then through childhood and puberty until we reach maturity in our adult bodies, so it is with our spiritual growth. Interestingly, it isn't until we reach near-adulthood that our spirituality really starts to explode. That's not to say young people can't have a deep relationship with the Lord; indeed, as evidenced by our look at children filled with God's Spirit, they can have a very clear leading from the Lord. But the maturity of spirituality and the subsequent use of your God-given gifts takes a lifetime.

YOUR PERSONALITY GIFTS

As your walk with the Lord causes you to shed more of yourself and in its place take on more of His clothing, you find that He gives you different attire in the form of gifts, talents, and skills, which are used to glorify Him.

Of course, your personality—that which makes you who you are—will help to define what gifts you have. Your personality is your inherent tendency toward certain thought patterns and reactions. Your personality can be strong, soft, reserved, abrasive, enthusiastic, philosophical, argumentative, analytical—you get the picture. Doubtless you know many different people, and each has a distinct personality.

Your personality is shaped in part by the genetic pool from which your biological parents drew and in part by the environment in which you grew up; nature vs. nurture. We all know families that have several children, none of whom look alike or act alike. Imagine how boring this world would be if God had only made a limited number of gene combinations from which our bodies could choose. Once again, He has shown us He is limitless!

Your innate tendencies toward how you receive, process, and interpret the world around you are what determine your personality. This in turn influences your spiritual motivational gift, or your primary, personality-determined gift.

I don't profess to be an expert on personality traits or spiritual gifts. Many excellent books have been written about spiritual gifts, supernatural gifts, and personality traits.[1] My curiosity is sparked more by our innate personalities; these define the gifts for which we have a tendency. This brief look will help you understand your ability to be still in God. You'll have a clearer grasp of how your personality gifts will influence your comfort level with the whole idea of stillness.

MOTIVATIONAL GIFTS

Take a look at the gifts listed in Romans 12:6–8:

> We have different gifts, according to the grace given us. If a man's gift is prophesying, let him use it in proportion to his faith. If it is serving, let him serve; if it is teaching, let him teach; if it is encouraging, let him encourage; if it is contributing to the needs of others, let him give generously; if it is leadership, let him govern diligently; if it is showing mercy, let him do it cheerfully.

The elementary spiritual gift in your life that motivates your actions is so intimately tied to your personality traits that you may not even see it as a gift. But the gift, used as you are walking in the Spirit and for God's purposes, gives you a ministry. Your motivational gift is so profound in you that you cannot function outside of it. In spiritual terms, it is your redeeming quality as a Christian—and a powerful tool for the kingdom of God.

Let's take a look at a few gifts that demonstrate what I mean. My husband's motivational gift is exhortation. Exhortation means he is, above all else, an encourager. He's upbeat, enthusiastic, and positive. He likes to pat people on the back, tell them they are doing a good job, or reinforce a positive action they have taken. He's the kind of guy that says, "You did a great job; I knew you could do it!" (By the way, he's a terrific guy to live with!)

I also have a very dear friend whose primary gift is service. She serves in a variety of ways—hospitably welcoming people into her home, volunteering in the community, and preparing food for church functions. Her deepest desire is to give of herself and talents to others. She gives unselfishly and without a need for reward. Her self-confidence is high because she lives unswervingly in the gifts the Lord has given her.

From these examples you see how the primary, most obvious gift influences every other area of life. For Peter, his exhortation defines how he reacts to just about every life circumstance: in an upbeat and encouraging way. My friend reacts with a servant's heart, looking for ways to graciously offer herself to others.

Why is it important to understand your spiritual gifts and personality traits as they relate to being still? Because if you are using your motivational gift as God has called you to, then you are free from nagging guilt for not doing certain other things people ask you to do. You can say no without an explanation because the use of your gifts is between you and God, not for others to assign or demand of you. In other words, when you are active in the gifts He has given you, you are free to "be still" in the gifts He hasn't given you.

Several years ago I was asked to help with the children's church ministry at our church, which takes place during our Sunday morning worship. The person asking me assumed that because I had children I would like to help organize other children. The reality is, I do not enjoy working with children. I adore my own children and believe all children are a treasure and a gift from the Lord, but that doesn't mean I have the patience or creativity to work with them. Did I feel guilty? No. Because I knew my gifts were better utilized in other places, I could say no to the request with a clear conscience.

GROWING GIFTS

In the parable of the talents in Matthew 25:14–30, Jesus tells us how we are to use the talents we are given. The talents He is talking about can be viewed as the monetary currency of those times, or they can be viewed as our English language interprets talents: personal gifts and skills.

This parable tells of how an apparently wealthy man was taking a journey. It seems it was likely going to be a long journey, perhaps several years. He wanted his money to multiply, not be left in a closet to accumulate dust. So he divided his wealth and entrusted it to three of his servants "according to their ability."

What does that mean? What ability? Did he know of their abilities from past experience? Was it his own projection of their abilities? Or was it simply hopeful thinking? My guess is that he knew the servant to whom he gave the least amount would likely not do anything with it.

The third servant had probably shown a previous propensity to withhold, to take what he was given and clutch it to his chest. He didn't want to let go of it, didn't want to risk investing it, feared it falling into the wrong hands, or, worse, losing it entirely. He was held hostage to a miserly spirit. This third servant seems to have had an identity crisis about his ability to do what his master asked of him, so he withdrew, isolated his talent, and probably skeptically watched the other two servants spending and investing their talents. I can imagine him snickering as he watched the money in the other servants' hands flow freely as they spent it on moneymaking ventures. But the sad joke was on him. The passage ends with his measly talent being given to the first, most productive servant, his fate being sealed with a degrading "worthless" title, and he being thrown like a piece of garbage out into the darkness, where there was "weeping and gnashing of teeth."

Ouch!

Do I see myself in this gripping story? I'm sad to say, yes. How about you? What talents, gifts, and skills has God blessed you with? Do you use them, invest them, spend them, give them away, freely furthering the investment God made in you to increase His kingdom? Or do you withhold them, fearful that if you use them they will disappear? Do you hide them, afraid if others find out about your gifts you will be taken advantage of? Do you have a miser's attitude about using your gifts?

God is not a withholding God. Nor is He shortsighted. He doesn't know how to hold back His blessings. He wants us to have it all, and He wants to give to us abundantly so that we and others can profit because of the use of our gifts. He wants us to purposefully multiply the talents He has given us and to have a plan of action in using, spending, and investing His gifts.

James 1:17 says, "Every good and perfect gift is from above, coming down from the Father of the heavenly lights, who does not change like shifting shadows." All gifts, which Paul tells us several times in 1 Corinthians to "eagerly desire," are available from God. I believe many of the analogies about nature and animals in the Bible were written because those images were around the authors as they wrote, and they drew on these mental pictures for means of comparison. So when James wrote the above verse, I picture him sitting by the light of the moon and stars, the "heavenly light," frantically trying to write out what was on his heart before the light was gone or obscured by clouds or shadows. He tells us that the gifts that come from God are permanent and impenetrable because they do not fade in the shadows of the world. That is how we need to view the gifts God has given us. God doesn't change with regard to the gifts He wants to give us, nor in His desire for us to use the gifts He has given us. It is our own humanness that gets in the way, casting a long shadow across our spiritual gifts.

I believe that every gift is available to every Christian in a certain measure during certain times of need. But I do not believe every gift will be manifested all the time in every Christian. There may be a time when, for a split second, a Christian mother is given discernment that her child is choking in the other room, or a Christian man suddenly speaks a relevant prophesy concerning his church. But neither may have the more permanent personality traits of either of these gifts.

In other words, some spiritual gifts may be available only at certain times of our lives, while others grow slowly, like fruit-bearing trees, taking years to produce a harvest.

When I first left high school, I felt a deep compassion for injured and ill people. My gift of mercy led me to nursing school, where I earned my degree and began working as a nurse at the age of twenty-two. I worked as an RN for eight years, but during the last year or two, other gifts began to manifest themselves in my spiritual life (even though I didn't lose my gift of mercy). Discernment offered me a look into the lives of women whom I counseled in a pregnancy center. Then a desire to write gripped me, and the feeling that I had something to teach through written words led me to release my nursing license. I've never regretted my decision. The Lord used my gift of mercy during those early years, but the subsequent gifts of administration and teaching have developed. My discernment has expanded to help me see the spiritual needs in other's lives so that I can minister to them. And I'm looking forward to what is in store for me next as I nurture a deeper growth with Him.

THE PROCESS

There is a progression not only of our faith but of our gifts. The more we use them and grow in them, the more we are blessed ourselves. We should desire to use our gifts, seeking out opportunities to minister to others, giving generously of what God has given to us. Second Corinthians 9:6–8 says,

Remember this: Whoever sows sparingly will also reap sparingly, and whoever sows generously will also reap generously. Each man should give what he has decided in his heart to give, not reluctantly or under compulsion, for God loves a cheerful giver.

This text is usually thought of in relation to giving money, but it isn't just about money. It's about giving your gifts, offering your time, volunteering yourself to serve God—cheerfully. When you give of yourself in your gifted areas, the blessing is triple: the person you've ministered to is blessed, you are blessed, and the Lord is blessed.

Every past experience, every past use of our gifts, prepares us for tomorrow. What happened in my life ten years ago, five years ago, one year ago, and even yesterday is determining what route I will take in the path before me tomorrow. And as my confidence and comfort increase while using the gifts God has given me, I become more effective in using them. And the more effective I am in my gifts, the more I am able to be still in them, quiet in spirit and motivation.

This process is only stopped by our inattentiveness to God's plan. Ah, spiritual attention deficit again. When we start to avoid God and evade His desired use of and action in our gifted areas, we lose the stillness in our lives. Just as an ocean takes days to settle to its normal rise and fall after a storm, we, too, take a long time to resettle after a stubborn skirmish with the Lord. It takes just a few minutes to work ourselves into a choppy, stormy scuffle with the Lord, and days for us to return to His calming influence.

NO EXPLANATIONS

It's a fine line we tread between using our gifts for God's glory and slipping into pride. Being still in our gifted areas means using them but not allowing them to become an area of self-gratification-seeking. It is dangerous to use God's talents for our own ambitious glory—ruin is sure to follow those who try to sidestep God's intended path for their lives. Matthew 6:1 issues this warning, "Be careful not to do your 'acts of righteousness' before men, to be seen by them. If you do, you will have no reward from your Father in heaven."

How do you avoid the pitfall of self-glory? Be aware of your human nature. When you're considering accepting a role that uses your gifts, ask yourself what your motivation is. Personally, I pray Psalm 139:23, "Search me, O God, and know my heart," when I'm testing the waters of a new responsibility or project. Is this for my glory or His? How will it utilize my gifts? How will my family be affected? He knows our hearts anyway, but sometimes we need to ask Him to reveal to us our own motivation: is it self-serving or God-serving?

The same can be said of any decision-making process. "Search me, O God, and know my heart." Reveal to me, affirm or deny, consent or object.

For a time I stopped going to church. A number of factors influenced this decision: discouragement about the direction our church was taking; fear of crowded places; disappointment that as a young, working mother I wasn't well represented among the leadership; anger about the way previous church situations had been handled. I'm sure you could write your own list of reasons why you would consider or indeed have stopped going to church for a while. People asked Peter where I was, and though he supported me in staying home for a time, he couldn't exactly explain it to others. I could barely explain it to *him*. I offered some excuses, but eventually just told him I needed to be alone; I needed to reaffirm my reasons for going to church, not so much my beliefs, but what my expectations were of a church body and of myself.

At the same time, however, I felt little remorse or guilt in staying home. Why? Because I asked God to "search" me, to test my motivation. Was I being sincere in seeking Him, or was I using my discouragement as a shield? I felt comforted by His permission to stay home and "be still." I also felt little compulsion to explain it to others. My spirituality, walk, and growth were between the Lord and me. Yes, I was accountable to my husband and the church leadership, but they were not responsible for my relationship with the Lord.

Only I was, and still am.

Jesus told us we are His sheep. David, because of his start in life as a young shepherd, did much of his comparative thinking in terms of sheep and their shepherd. (I like to think he chose sheep as an analogy not because of their stupidity, but because of their willingness to be led.) If we are indeed "the people of his pasture" (Psalm 95:7), where do we turn when we need direction? To the other sheep? I hope not! The obvious answer is the Lord, the Great Shepherd. I find it distressing to see so many people adopt the herd mentality and attach themselves to the words or actions of other mortal "sheep." I agree the Lord has given us gifted leaders to whom we are spiritually accountable and to whom we can turn for wise counsel. But to whom are we answerable in the end? Our almighty God. I don't want to stand before Him in glory and say, "But back in 1985 so and so, who had spiritual credits as long as my arm, said I should . . ." No thanks. I will take the full weight of my own spiritual health on my own shoulders. I alone am responsible for my walk with the Lord.

During the time I excused myself from church, this "no apology, no explanation" approach worked for me. Not that I would suggest that this is a prescription for your situation. Yes, I was concerned about what it said to my children. Yes, I missed the community of believers, but this time I took alone to be still in God's presence returned me to my true spirituality—my authentic spirituality.

AUTHENTIC SPIRITUALITY

Genuine faith is dependent on no one but yourself. That doesn't mean we don't need other people or that we should live independently in our faith. Indeed, the Great Commission is to spread the gospel; we can't do that if we are completely self-absorbed in our faith. We are called to not only develop a personal walk with the Lord but to invite others on the same journey.

What I mean by self-directed faith is that your spiritual growth and maturity are between you and the Lord. In *Woman of Influence*, Pam Farrel puts it this way: "Because the goal is intimacy, not legalistic ritual, every woman is free to develop her relationship with God uniquely. The blend of ingredients may change with time or circumstance."[2] As Farrel says, it's through prayer and developing an intimate relationship with Him that you gain independence from the herd mentality. Jesus Christ died to save *you* (and everyone else in the herd), but His desire is for you to follow Him because He is trustworthy, not because everyone else says it's a good thing to do. And in this assurance you can be still, not propelled along in the middle of a spiritual stampede.

Another problem with the spiritual herd mentality is that we hear and read so much teaching about how to do things the "right" way that we lose sight of the "why."

A couple of years ago I felt called to fast and pray—something I hadn't done in a number of years under the excuse of pregnancies, breast-feeding, and low blood sugar. But I knew the Lord wanted all of me—all of my attention. I read a few books and leaflets to organize myself to fast the "right" way. As my anxiety increased over not being "allowed" to have coffee in the morning, I lost sight of what I was trying to accomplish—simply to have a pure and intimate time with the Lord. As I was discussing my impending fast with Him, I suddenly saw in my mind's eye the Lord sitting quietly on His throne, shaking His head with a patient half-smile on His face. He seemed to say, "My dear child, don't you know that it's your whole heart, uninterrupted time, and uncluttered soul I desire? Don't concern yourself with what is right for other people, concern yourself with what is right for you."

"Of course, Lord. Why didn't I think of that?" Because I got too bogged down in doing it man's way instead of God's way.

First Corinthians 7:23–24 reminds us, "You were bought at a price; do not become slaves of men. Brothers, each man, as responsible to God, should remain in the situation God called him to."

What other things do we as Christians strive to do the right way—the commonly accepted way? Worship, prayer, Bible study, devotional times? These "acts of spirituality," as I call them, are just that, "acts." Do they in and of themselves show or prove our spiritual level? You may be able to fool others if you "know the talk and walk the walk," but God knows your heart. He knows if your motivation is pure and if you are desirous of a true relationship with Him, or if you're pretending. And once again, you are ultimately answerable to Him. You may fool others, but you won't fool Him, and in the end you shortchange yourself.

Being held by the binding ropes of "spirituality bondage," the need to prove your faith prevents you from being spiritually still. The tight restrictions of bondage disallow the free movement of a still spirit. Remember the "be still" word picture of a carefree, graceful ballet dancer in a meadow? Now imagine her arms reaching out to grab other people's attention, "Look at me! Look how beautifully I move! Isn't my dance of spirituality lovely?" How unbecoming. Her self-serving dance isn't attractive to anyone because it has fallen flat on the grass at her feet instead of reaching to the heavens. But if her dance returns to glorifying God and being still in God's presence, her authenticity is obvious. The motivation of your spiritual dance must be God-directed, not an attention grabber for mankind.

When your motivation is driven by authenticity, a genuine desire to serve God alone and no one else, you become a real person doing real things. Your confidence in your ability to serve God in your gifted areas grows because you are quiet in His Spirit. Your effectiveness increases, because, in the stillness of your being, you are allowing God to be God.

Stillness in Action

I'd like to give you permission to stay home from church for a time, or your job for a day or two. Not that you need my permission—you certainly don't—but I do want to encourage you to seek God's answer in staying home from church for a predetermined amount of time. Just be sure your motivation is clear. Even for those who adore going to church each week, I challenge you to try staying home.

Staying home from church doesn't mean you can catch up on housework, or prepare the noon meal, or care for a sick child. No, it means literally being still for the whole time you would normally be in church. Make yourself a cup of tea, take your Bible and journal, and settle in a comfortable place. Even if you fall asleep or allow your mind to wander, the point is that you are being still in yourself, in your home (a place that is probably in perpetual motion most of the time), and in God's presence.

MEMORY VERSE

"Do not conform any longer to the pattern of this world, but be transformed by the renewing of your mind. Then you will be able to test and approve what God's will is—his good, pleasing and perfect will."

ROMANS 12:2

Being Quiet

"He will take great delight in you,
he will quiet you with his love,
he will rejoice over you with singing."

Z E P H A N I A H   3 : 1 7

While writing this chapter, even as I looked at my computer screen and thought about how to describe being restive and quiet, distracting noise seeped into my office. The vacuum cleaner whooshed downstairs, the dog's tags jingled on her collar as she settled into a spot next to me, and Jordan danced and sang in his room. I felt the tension building in my upper arms and neck. How could I possibly write about quiet when it was a forgotten and unpracticed discipline in my own home? It seemed a dichotomy that my inner stress was building to a crescendo while I attempted to write about peace and quiet.

Then I remembered another time when stress weighted my shoulders. Peter was gone for a week, having left on a Friday. Usually in his absences I cut all extraneous activities down to "must do's." For some reason that weekend I was scheduled to host, co-host, or serve (I occasionally work for a caterer) at four different parties over three days' time. By the following Tuesday I felt tired, fragmented, and discouraged. Work deadlines were highlighted in red on my calendar, and I had several school activities I needed to attend. The house looked a wreck and the laundry smelled pretty ripe. I had a few open hours Tuesday afternoon to work, and though feeling very uncreative, I marched into my office and switched on the computer. The box emitted a series of grating beeps. It was a noise I knew only too well: harddrive failure. I cried, not because I might have lost anything stored (I always back everything up), but because the word "failure" seemed to tear at my already shredded confidence. I felt as though my computer was speaking to me personally. Failure: failure to organize my life; failure to be a good mommy when Peter was away; failure to complete my work projects; failure to keep the house neat and tidy. I was having a serious confidence crisis, and even my computer noticed!

Instead of taking those two hours to write, I hastily disconnected the computer, tossed it on the front seat of my car, and drove to the computer store half an hour from home. During the next four days, discouragement and anxiety kept tapping me on the shoulder. But every time I felt it starting to weigh me down, I recited Psalm 46:10. And each time I said the words "be still" I felt as though the Lord was telling me literally to be still, actually to go lie down. I complied. At first I felt guilty about lying down when there were so many "should be doing" thoughts churning in my mind. But the impression was so strong that the Lord wanted me to be physically still, that not to be still would be disobedience. At the end of the week, feeling more rested and at peace than I had in weeks, I called the computer store to get the report on my computer. The technician sounded a bit confused. "Well," he said, "I've switched your computer on and off about fifty times and it boots up perfectly each time. I've checked all your systems and everything seems to be fine." Feeling somewhat embarrassed, I muttered my thanks and hung up.

Once again God used a specific attention-getter to remind me to return my focus to Him. Despite—and likely because of—all the time I spent resting, I completed my household tasks at the end of the week with energy and enthusiasm, plus I still met all my writing deadlines on time.

It may seem contradictory to rest when faced with so many home/work activities that need attention. But the Lord helped me switch my personal drive to complete everything—my own "hard drive"—into neutral. He wanted me to coast along in Him, not attempt to gather, gain, and store energy on my own.

RESTING

The simple activities of daily life, the maintaining of household chores, work, children, pets, other family members, friends—all these require energy. But having accessible energy is dependent on enough rest and quiet.

I'm reminded of the precursor to Jesus feeding the five thousand. Mark 6:30–32 says,

> The apostles gathered around Jesus and reported to him all they had done and taught. Then, because so many people were coming and going that they did not even have a chance to eat, he said to them, "Come with me by yourselves to a quiet place and get some rest." So they went away by themselves in a boat to a solitary place.

I can picture the apostles clamoring around Jesus, excitedly relaying their reports, but being constantly interrupted by other people. Maybe they showed their frustration at not being able to complete a sentence or thought. Jesus knew his disciples needed a break, a rest, a time to regather energy. I can imagine Him pulling them into a huddle and saying, "Come, let's get on the boat, just us, where you can eat, rest, and be quiet. Then you'll have the energy to face other people."

The place where they landed their boat must have required a bit of a journey, because the people who ran to meet Jesus and the disciples arrived before the boat did. During the sailing, they probably ate, slept, and talked quietly one-on-one with Jesus. And a good thing, too! Imagine the energy they needed to minister to and feed five thousand men, plus women and children! First, they helped the people get settled on the hillside, then they passed around the baskets of fish and bread. Afterward, they cleaned up after everyone had eaten, filling the baskets again with scraps. They must have traversed the grassy hillside dozens of times! Imagine if they hadn't had that time of rest beforehand. The work would have been physically taxing. Emotionally they may have felt resentful of the hungry people. Spiritually they would have been empty with no discernment to see the people's spiritual needs. But instead, they were prepared with all the resources required to feed thousands of people because they had rested with the Lord *first*, and not waited until their reserves were completely depleted. The Lord no doubt recognized that their reserve levels were dangerously low before the miracle. He literally sequestered them for a time of rejuvenation.

He wants us to listen as keenly as the disciples did when He suggested the boat trip. They didn't say, "Wait a minute, Lord, I want to finish repairing the sails first" or "I need to have a snack first" or "I really want to talk with this person first." Yet don't we do this all the time? Run, chase, dash, rush, and hustle through various activities while we furtively glance behind us, hoping to catch a glimpse of Jesus on the horizon hurrying to keep up with us? And all He wants is that we slow down enough to match Him stride for stride.

When we fall into step with Him, we may find there are times when He seems to be moving painfully slow, forcing us to take a look at every detail of the landscape around us. Other times He may grab our hand and spirit us along at breakneck speed, barely giving us a chance to catch our breath. At still other times, He stops altogether and either gathers us in His protective arms or stands quietly at our side. The point is that we need to be going in the same direction and speed as He is—regardless of our missteps, stumbles, trips, and strides along the way. As the apostles learned, our walk can only be true and completely matched stride for stride with Him when we are rested first.

Sometimes we whine and complain to Him, "But I'm tired, Lord." And what is His response? What is the only thing He can say? "Come to me . . . and I will give you rest" (Matthew 11:28).

SPIRITUAL REST

The Lord felt so strongly about His people taking time to rest that he issued a command in Exodus 34:21: "Six days you shall labor, but on the seventh day you shall rest; even during the plowing season and harvest you must rest." Why did the Lord feel it necessary to point this out? One of the resultant curses after Adam and Eve's sin was they would have to toil and sweat and scratch the earth for their existence. In Genesis 3:17 it says, "Cursed is the ground because of you; through painful toil you will eat of it." Then in verse 19: "By the sweat of your brow you will eat your food." The physical and mental labor we exert every day is a result of original sin.

Yet God commands a reprieve each week. "On the seventh day you shall rest." I believe His command means to take time away from the work force. A time to regather physical energy. A time to be fed spiritually. A time to embrace family and spend quality hours with one another. I'll admit to this verse being somewhat open to interpretation, but let me relay a little story to you and then you can decide what kind of rest the Lord desires of you on the "seventh day."

A very dear friend of mine is a struggling single parent. She receives no support from the child's father, nor does she accept government aid. She developed a catering and house-cleaning business over a two-year period to meet her expenses, and she unswervingly accepted God's promise of provision for the fatherless and the widow. But in fulfilling her responsibilities, she frequently had to work on Sundays. She'd go to church, dash home, settle her child with the sitter, and rush off to work the rest of the day. Then she began to feel convicted. It wasn't any one person or any particular incident that pricked her conscience, but she started to wonder if she could completely trust the Lord to provide for her needs if she stopped working on Sundays. Would He be faithful? Would her clients understand? Would it be a testimony to others? Would she pick up enough work on the other days to meet her financial obligations?

The answer is a simple yes to each of those concerns. Her conviction and God's compassion cojoined, making it possible for her to turn down Sunday work. God honored her decision. Plenty of work came in during the weekdays, she continued to meet her financial responsibilities, and her customers affirmed her. Her Sundays became a time of spiritual rejuvenation rather than a race to get her sermon fix for the week.

My friend felt convicted, she acted, she waited, and she found God faithful. Now, I can't tell you how you need to keep your seventh day a day of rest. That's between you, the Lord, your family, and your beliefs. I don't write on Sundays, but I do occasionally work for a caterer. I always check with my husband first about working on a Sunday, and if he's away I won't accept a job on the Sabbath.

I see the seventh-day rest as a time to review the week, spiritually and physically. And, as I covered in the previous chapter, because I am dependent on and responsible to only the Lord for my spiritual growth, I consider Sunday a day of confirmation. This may or may not come through a Sunday service. But if I am "resting" spiritually, then I am vulnerable and open to God's confirmation of something in my life. Perhaps He'll confirm something I may have prayed about during the week. Or maybe He'll verify my taking time with my family, or allow me a glimpse of His awesome creation while enjoying a horseback ride in the woods. This time of reflection reminds me to take Psalm 116:7 to heart: "Be at rest once more, O my soul, for the Lord has been good to you."

God designed Sunday rest as an antidote to our perpetual spiritual attention deficit. A whole day set aside for us to shed the layers of "doing" from our exhausted beings and don a fresh, crisp, godly perspective.

EMOTIONAL REST

With God's uncluttered perspective, we can begin to see our lives the way He does. When we are open and vulnerable because we have rested physically and spiritually, God's voice takes on a timbre we might not have heard in our otherwise clanging-cymbal lives.

Ecclesiastes 4:6 reads, "Better one handful with tranquillity than two handfuls with toil and chasing after the wind." What a statement of simplicity! King Solomon, a man who *knew* the heart of God, who owned every material possession imaginable, who was exceptionally wealthy—even by today's standards—still recognized the importance of reducing personal clutter. The Lord allowed Solomon to have it all, to experience life to its fullest, yet Solomon came back to just one thought in this verse: Less is more.

Solomon was talking about an inner tranquillity. A peacefulness of spirit. A contentment with work done. A realization that inner calm feels so much healthier than a scattered, fragmented life.

Solomon's trademark, "a chasing after the wind," is such a vivid picture of our attention deficit lives. We chase after something that we can't see, can't confine, and can't control. This futile chase is without any guarantees in return. What a waste of energy! Solomon knew from experience that it was better to have half as much and a sedate demeanor than twice as much with a flustered life.

Not only is a scattered life physically draining, it is emotionally exhausting. The proverbial finger in too many pies stretches you and leaves you with a bad taste in your mouth. Inevitably we invest a great deal of hope, expectation, and desire into our various pursuits.

I'm reminded of a time when I (notice the operative word "I") wanted to start a small group for my horseback-riding friends. I had grandiose ideas of meeting once a month and talking about our horses and our various riding disciplines. I planned, made calls, and had hopes for this group. I invested myself emotionally in making us bond and grow together. Simply put, my self-esteem became so wrapped up in the "success" of the group that I felt deeply hurt when it didn't turn out the way I'd planned. Other people's lives were too busy to commit to a group meeting. In hindsight, I see that to meet formally as a group would have completely changed the dynamics of the friendships I had with those people. But at the time, because I cared fondly about each one of them, I thought we should be organized about seeing one another regularly. I likely would have spoiled the casual, catch-up-when-we-can, no-strings-attached nature of my friendships. I was trying to make them into something they weren't.

Yes, I felt disappointed it didn't work out, but I learned a valuable lesson. If I had worked half as hard and just called each one once a month for a quick check-in, I would have accomplished twice as much and not wasted so much energy in trying to create a group atmosphere. My pursuit of establishing a horseback-riding group was a chasing after the wind.

Once again I felt drawn back to the Lord for my emotional well to be topped off. I had lost precious drops of emotional energy on a worthless endeavor. I needed to restore my emotional reserves. How? Like a revolving door that keeps bringing its occupant back out to the street, this occupant had to revolve out of my own inner desires and return to God's path for me.

Jeremiah 6:16: "Stand at the crossroads and look; ask for the ancient paths, ask where the good way is, and walk in it, and you will find rest for your souls." I should have taken this advice myself. Stand, look, ask twice, walk—then you will find rest.

Let's look at this verse a little more in depth.

First, you have to stop and stand still. Quiet enough to hear God's voice in a whisper or a shout. Still enough to feel His presence in and around you. Calm enough to perceive His directives. Discerning enough to weed out and toss on the refuse pile what is not of Him.

Second, you have to look. Look at the landscape around you— hills, valleys, straightaways, rocks, and fields. Search for hidden land mines and stumbling blocks. Be introspective and consider all the demands of your life. View the options of routes and avenues. Drink it all in to enable yourself to make an informed decision about the available paths.

Third, you must ask for direction. Not once, but twice, for confirmation. Ask with the knowledge of how God has worked in the past. Search the Scriptures for "the ancient paths." The most worn and popular route may not be the "good way." Question God for what His good and perfect will is for the route He wants you to take.

Fourth, take a step. Walk with faith on the road He points you toward. Stride forward with confidence and conviction. March out with a clear conscience, knowing that you have stopped, looked, asked, and only then, acted.

Fifth, He will grant you rest. No more fruitless searching, no more aimless wanderings. No more taking another and another and another spin in the revolving door. This formula, if you can call it that—stop, look, ask, and walk—is what will produce the inner calm, assurance, and rest you so desire in your emotional, spiritual, and physical life. It's that simple!

Joshua 21 talks about the division of allotted land, towns, and pastureland according to what the Lord had commanded the Israelites through Moses (it adds up to forty-eight towns, each surrounded by pasturelands—not just a few acres). As a result of the Israelites following through on the commitment Moses had made, verse 44 says, "The Lord gave them rest on every side, just as He had sworn to their forefathers." Rest on every side. No bickering about boundaries, no fighting about ownership. Each Levite in each of the forty-eight towns was content and at rest. Each Israelite took possession of the land the Lord had promised to their forefathers.

Everyone had enough land and felt content with their allotment. Imagine that kind of restfulness! The Levites and Israelites were granted peace; *complete*, comprehensive peace. Inner and outer, personally and collectively. What a wonderful, tranquil time it must have been. And it was all according to what God had promised them. His desire for us is no less. Of course He wants us to experience "rest on every side." Rest within ourselves and rest with those around us. Rest spiritually, emotionally, and physically.

PHYSICAL REST

To be successful at keeping a tranquil spirit and even-keeled emotions, your body must have physical rest. Look at Psalm 23 with me: "The Lord is my shepherd, I shall not be in want. He makes me lie down in green pastures." Stop there. First, God is the provider of everything. He anticipates our needs before we do and His provision is complete. As much or as little as we need—when, how, and where we need it. We don't need to say to Him, "I want." We no longer have "wants." We have requests and needs. Wanting implies self-centeredness, while "not being in want" confirms God's faithful provision.

The second verse is even more profound when you realize in this analogy to sheep: the Lord has us "lie down in green pastures." Not eat, graze, wander about, and bleat loudly to those around us. No, lie down. The lying down implies that not only are we well fed and satisfied, we are safe. We are resting. We are ruminating on His provision. We are regaining energy. In the safety of His green pastures, we are peacefully quiet, resting under the watchful and protective eye of our Great Shepherd. Without the Lord's protective eye, we become muddled, as Matthew describes: "When he saw the crowds, he had compassion on them, because they were harassed and helpless, like sheep without a shepherd"(9:36).

When David wrote the Twenty-third Psalm, he sensed the sheep's need to rest as a priority over the other provisions listed in the psalm. He knew the sheep needed strength to move from pasture to pasture; they needed shade during the hot midday as relief from their woolly coats; they needed to feel safe before they could sleep.

Phillip Keller writes, "It is significant that to be at rest there must be a definite sense of freedom from fear, tension, aggravations, and hunger. The unique aspect of the picture is that it is only the sheep-man himself who can provide release from these anxieties. It all depends upon the diligence of the owner whether or not his flock is free of disturbing influences."[1]

Once the flock is worry-free, the sheep, or in this case, His followers, are revived. After the lying down and the leading beside still waters follows "He restores my soul." Part of His provision is a restored soul; a renewed and refreshed spirit as a result of lying down, of resting. Bodily rest augments a restored soul.

At the beginning of this chapter, I gave an example of how the Lord forced me to physically lie down every time I was impressed with the verse "Be still, and know that I am God." It was a sacrifice of my time to do that. I had to relinquish my plans, lists, and agenda to Him. I had to offer Him all I had—my physical being. Romans 12:1 says, "Offer your bodies as living sacrifices, holy and pleasing to God—this is your spiritual act of worship." My bodily sacrifice of resting was an act of worship? Lying down had been not only an act of obedience during those days but also a form of worship. Why? Because I valued my body and its resources enough to take care of it, to rest it when God told me to.

The Lord generally leaves our physical rest up to our discretion. If you can exist on only five or six hours of sleep a night, my guess is that is exactly what you take. You get by with the bare minimum. But studies show that many adults are functioning in a sleep-deprived state. When you are sleep-deprived, other areas are compromised. Some people get confused, others yawn through the day, some fall asleep at stoplights, some nod off after lunch. Is this spiritual worship? Taking advantage of our bodies? Depriving them of needed sleep? No. Our bodies are a gift to be honored, cared for, and ultimately used for God's glory, while sleeping and while awake.

ACTIVE QUIET

Active quiet. Sounds like a contradiction. Once you are active, moving about through space, you can't help but make noise—right? Yes, but active quiet takes place once you have fully adopted stillness as a part of your life. Out of personal stillness, action can take place that does not compromise your inner quiet. Let me explain.

A very dear friend of mine, Beth, was with me when I gave birth to Jordan. I had asked her to join Peter and me during the birth because I wanted her to take pictures of my labor and delivery. She has a very quiet spirit, and I knew I could count on her unflustered approach should I feel out of control during labor. My labor was fast and furious; I never even made it to the birthing room. Jordan was ten days overdue and he wanted out!! Peter lovingly cradled our new, big boy (he weighed 9 lbs., 1 oz.), and the doctor waited for the placenta to be delivered. He told me to gently push, but when I did a tremendous gush of blood followed. The doctor, face strained, motioned to the nurse to ask Peter and Beth to leave. Peter, still tenderly cradling Jordan, obediently followed the nurse out of the room, but I clung to Beth's hand.

"Let her stay," I whispered. The doctor gave me a dark nod. I could feel blood draining from my body. I felt scared. I started to tremble. Then the doctor reached deep inside to remove the portion of the placenta that had apparently torn from the bulk. I screamed. I flailed against his hand. A stream of curses poured from my mouth. I cried gulping, gasping breaths. The pain shot from my pelvis all the way to my head and back down my legs. Excruciating isn't descriptive enough. Beth gently and tenderly leaned across my shoulders and focused her eyes on my blurry ones. "What do you want me to do?" she asked.

"Sing to me," I sobbed. She was instantly filled with the Holy

Spirit, because the very next breath from her mouth carried the song "The joy of the Lord is my strength, the joy of the Lord is my strength. . . ."

I took a deep, tearing breath. The anguish began to ebb away. The doctor wasn't quite done, but I could feel God's very presence come over me and quiet me. I felt a peace infiltrate into every corner of the room. My body stopped shaking, my tears dried, and I even smiled at Beth. I whispered my thanks to her just as the doctor asked the nurse to start cleaning up the mess.

That's active quiet. Beth's actions, her willingness to share her quiet nature to minister to me, acted like a healing oil on my head. If she had panicked, shown fear, turned away in disgust, or become flustered, her presence would have been useless to me. Instead, her peacefulness and restful nature overflowed to embrace me in my need for quiet. Through Beth the Holy Spirit restored my physical strength and my spiritual focus.

In those moments I learned that quietness is something you can give away. You can have it and practice it in your life, and if you have an excess you can distribute it to others without diminishing your own peacefulness. Others see it in your life, and they are drawn to it.

In her book *Wilderness Time*, Emilie Griffin describes inner peacefulness this way: "It is the sense of inner harmony, of knowing ourselves in an easygoing and self-forgiving way that becomes possible through the life of grace. The spiritual disciplines of guidance, submission, and service all have something to do with developing this inner confidence or peace."[2]

You know the kind of women we're talking about here. In a word, they are serene. Despite several children vying for their attention, or the fact that they are facing dramatic life choices, they carry a tranquillity and obvious God-given peacefulness around them like a cloak. You just want to reach out and have a piece of it.

The good news is you can. And you're already well on your way to having it.

Look at the well-known, actively quiet woman of the Bible: the Proverbs 31 woman. I know, we all sometimes feel this "woman of noble character" ideal is completely unattainable. I like to look at a few choice phrases from verses 10 to 31 to help grasp the nature of this God-fearing woman:

Her husband has full confidence in her.

She works with diligent hands.

She provides food for her family.

She sets about her work vigorously.

She opens her arms to the poor.

She makes coverings and linen garments.

She watches over her house.

She is clothed with strength and dignity.

She offers faithful instruction with wisdom.

How does she have the energy to do all this? The answer is found in verse 30: "A woman who fears the Lord is to be praised."

King Lemuel recognized that all these qualities in this noble woman were a result of her fear of the Lord.

Does it say she fretted about all the tasks she needed to accomplish? Or complained about her responsibilities and obligations? No, the entire passage implies that she went about her work with energy, enthusiasm, love, happiness, mercy, discernment, and intelligence. As a matter of fact, the only thing it says about her words is, "She speaks with wisdom, and faithful instruction is on her tongue."

This woman personifies active quiet. She is busy all right. But she goes about her business with conviction. She doesn't appear to get flustered or sidetracked. It certainly would be a waste of her energy to have a fragmented approach to her day! She stays focused on her jobs. And when she does speak, I imagine she ponders for a moment, searching for a godly, wise response, then provides a succinct, correct answer.

In verses 11 and 12 it says, "Her husband has full confidence in her. . . . She brings him good." Would her husband have complete and uncompromised confidence in her if she bickered, argued, fretted, acted insecurely, or was indecisive? I don't think so.

I am convinced her active life is attained because she has a still, God-fearing spirit. Her quiet but confident demeanor is a result of using the gifts and talents God has given her in an appropriate manner. She doesn't question, she just does.

Another person from the Bible who didn't question but acted was Noah.

Noah is an interesting study in God-fearing. Imagine the ridicule people must have tossed at him. I can even imagine his own family desperately wanting to trust him but quietly concerned for his mental health, pulling him aside and asking, "But Noah, are you *sure*? Are you really sure?" It's not like the Lord instructed him to build something that wouldn't be obvious to others. You can't hide an ark in your garage. But Noah's conviction was so strong that he shouldered the mockery from the dubious onlookers and gathered more wood.

Genesis 6:22 says, "Noah did everything just as God commanded him to." We aren't told if he questioned God; we aren't told if he fasted and prayed for exact directions; we aren't told if he felt scared, uncertain, or frenzied. What we are told is that Noah was obedient right through the process.

Noah's lack of words is an extreme example of active quiet. He acted on faith and went about the work with conviction and confidence. He likely wasn't silent throughout the building of the ark, but it's also likely that if he was the sort to complain and question, God wouldn't have chosen him to be the general contractor in the first place.

What can we learn from all three of these examples? Being quiet is having confidence in your actions. It is an assurance that when we are unwaveringly still before God we have the energy to perform the actions for which He has equipped us. Initially, while we need to regather our energies and refocus on His direction, there may be times when He calls us to literally be still and take a physical, emotional, and spiritual rest. But once we've laid to rest the extraneous clutter clinging to our spirit and added in its stead God's peaceful calm, we can start to act again in His quiet assurance.

Stillness in Action

Charles Swindoll writes in his book *Intimacy With the Almighty*,

> Yet, I am more convinced than ever that there is no way you and I can move toward a deeper, intimate relationship with our God without protracted times of stillness, which includes one of the rarest of all experiences: absolute silence."[3]

Schedule a day for a "talking fast." No, not a day of rapid conversations, but a day (or half a day, or a couple of hours) of no talking. Your listening skills will improve, but more importantly, you will find that your thoughts automatically turn to prayerful conversations in your mind. He is the only one that can hear your thoughts anyway, so when you consciously stop talking out loud, He is the only one you can talk to. Let the answering machine pick up the phone, prepare your family (you can always write notes if necessary, but it does work better if you are alone), and record your day of quiet in your journal.

MEMORY VERSE

"My soul finds rest in God alone; my salvation comes from him."

PSALM 62:1

CHAPTER FIVE

Being Watchful

"But as for me, I watch in hope for the Lord,
I wait for God my Savior; my God will hear me."

MICAH 7:7

My mother grew up with horses. As a child she would saddle up her pony in the morning, drop her sack lunch into the saddlebag, and explore her small town's woods and roads until the sun touched the treetops on its way down. After she married my father, she didn't have a horse for a number of years—three young children and a new business took precedence. I remember when her dream to have a horse again came true.

She bought Charlie Brown for two hundred dollars. In my six-year-old mind, I thought his palomino golden coat sparkled like the sun itself. I'd tenderly brush and pat his neck and shoulders every chance I got. I *lived* for the days when Mom would take me for even just a short ride. I'd pester her as she saddled up, "When you come back from your ride, can I ride him, *please, please!*" She'd nod, gather the reins, hop up into the saddle, and amble off down the road. I'd sigh, breathing in the last whiff of horsehair in their wake.

Then I'd go sit on the front lawn and wait.

It seemed interminable so many times, to wait and watch for Mom and Charlie to return. But the wait was filled with anticipation. Not a restless, anxiety-filled expectancy; it was a content wait. Because I knew every time Mom returned she'd give me a ride. Every time. If I was waiting and ready, she would grant me the free-spirited joy she knew I felt whenever I rode. During those watchful hours, I'd lie back and gaze at listless clouds overhead. I'd chew on a clover stem. I'd pretend I was a wild horse and gallop around whinnying. One time I remember the sun warming me into sleep on the soft grass. My ears always tuned to far-off noises, eventually I'd hear the distant ring of Charlie's shoes on the road, briskly clip-clopping along. That's all I needed. I'd jump up and race down the road as fast as my little legs could churn. Mom would always greet me with a smile, "Been waiting, have you?" Then she'd reach down to my outstretched hand, pull me up, help guide my scrambling foot into the stirrup, and slide my body behind her saddle onto the back of Charlie.

And we'd be off.

Utter, complete happiness for one little girl. (No wonder I still love and own horses!)

These memories of time spent waiting for my mom remind me of how God our Father has this same happy, watchful anticipation for what He can give us and do in our lives! If only we can learn to wait with expectant joy, knowing His purposes for us will give us absolute contentment.

WAITING FOR THE LORD

Watchfully waiting for the Lord is one of the many faces of being still. It seems He is holding up a stoplight to signal our stillness. He keeps the red light on while we frustratingly wait and wait and wait, one foot tapping impatiently on the accelerator.

Waiting for the Lord to answer a prayer can seem to take forever. Yet to Him a thousand years is but a day. God simply does not operate by our interpretation or standard of time. The second-hand-sweep to us is constant, motivating us to action. But God doesn't live by a clock. Time is insignificant. He acts, speaks, and answers prayers according to His own plan. To Him it's all one big continuum. It's like a timeline map in *National Geographic*; the Lord sees time from the beginning all the way to the end. Our brief lives on earth are just a small dot on that line. Not that we're inconsequential (our lives do have great consequence to Him) but we are merely punctuation marks along that line.

It's important to understand this. Waiting for the Lord to give a green light to our requests is His nature—because He is the beginning and the end, He knows our requests will be met before the end. Our nature, on the other hand, is impetuous impatience. Imagine how demanding and assuming we would become if all our requests were met immediately. There is *always* something to be learned in the waiting. Perhaps we need to learn to relinquish control to Him, perhaps we need to repent of a sin, perhaps there is more work to be done in other people's lives before our prayer can come to fruition. Regardless of the reason why we wait, we are required to wait.

ANTICIPATION

Waiting builds a sense of anticipation. Somehow the reward seems sweeter when you have been preparing for the answer for a while. Waiting builds an excitement about how your prayers will be answered. Savoring the possibilities of how the Lord will respond is like tasting chocolate. Your mouth waters, you roll it around on your tongue, then you taste and test the texture and feel. We do the same with potential different answers from God. We try them on for size, play out scenarios in our minds, and think about how we will feel about His possible answers. Waiting, watching, and ruminating force us to stay focused on Him. We grow in our faith as our dependency on Christ becomes completely real and as we realize we have no control over the wait.

The Lord knows we feel unnerved while waiting. It can make us feel scattered and fragmented. Psalm 27:14 offers us guidance: "Wait for the Lord; be strong and take heart and wait for the Lord." When I read this in the midst of waiting for the Lord's answer or waiting for Him to act, it reminds me to stand up straight and confidently square my shoulders. It reminds me to place my hand over my heart, pledging my faith in God.

Luke 2:41–52 relays the account of when the twelve-year-old Jesus stayed behind in Jerusalem after the Feast of the Passover. His mother and father searched for Him for three days and scolded Him when they finally found Him, "Son, why have you treated us like this? Your father and I have been anxiously searching for you." Can you imagine the wait that Mary endured while searching for her son during those three days? I'm sure she cried, prayed, and worried. Her thoughts may have been: *I gave birth to the Son of God and I've gone and* misplaced *Him!* She may have wondered about God's plan and timing for Jesus, perhaps thinking, *Maybe my son's work is done; maybe He's about to complete God's plan on earth and I've* missed *it!* I'm sure her wait to locate Jesus seemed an eternity, because even though she was the biological mother of the Son of God, she was still a worried, anxious, devoted, scared, and concerned mother first.

Sounds like me!

But there was something for her to learn in the waiting and something for us to learn by reading about her wait. Faith and trust come to mind. Faith that the Lord God always has our best interests at heart while we wait. Trust that His divine will is the best alternative for our lives during our wait.

UNDIVIDED HEARTS

I'm also reminded of how the Israelites followed the cloud of the Lord during the years of their wanderings. They had been commanded that when the cloud moved they were to follow it and when it stopped they were to encamp and stay put until the cloud moved again. In Numbers 9:22 it says, "Whether the cloud stayed over the tabernacle for two days or a month or a year, the Israelites would remain in camp and not set out; but when it lifted, they would set out."

Sometimes I think it would be easier if we all had a cloud of direction in our lives like the Israelites did. There is no doubt about their occasional grumblings, misgivings, and impatience, but when it came right down to choice, they had none but to follow the ever-present cloud. They simply had to wait for the Lord's direction. Certainly there may have been some who defiantly decided to strike out on their own, braving the desert, certain they could find their own way to the Promised Land. But when they separated themselves from the security of the group, they divided themselves from God himself.

As the Israelites learned, God's way is along the path of waiting. And we are usually just as impatient as the Israelites were. We may stand before two roads and pray about which direction to take. His answer may well be, "Why don't you sit and have a rest first?" He may want us to ponder on the choice and pray, "Teach me your way, O Lord, and I will walk in your truth; give me an undivided heart, that I may fear your name" (Psalm 86:11). Undivided heart? A heart that is focused solely on God's way.

An undivided heart keeps us from second-guessing God. Much of the time we can't possibly understand why God does what He does. But a heart that is faithfully focused on the truth doesn't need to try to figure out God's ways. Trying to confine God only limits us.

I tend to do a lot of second-guessing, particularly in my work. I wonder if I should send a manuscript to an editor on a particular day so she gets it at the beginning of the week when perhaps she is feeling fresher. Or I spend days speculating about whether to call an editor with a question. I agonize about what words to use in a cover letter. I waste an awful lot of energy talking myself into and out of so many things!

And what is this? Simple unbelief. A divided heart means I'm not watching God but, instead, have my focus turned inward. My heart is divided between trusting God to take the words He has given me to use them as He desires and my need to control and know what will happen to my written words.

LOSING CONTROL

Did I just use the "C" word? Control. Ouch! Why does that word make me cringe? Because I know the struggles so many of us battle while relinquishing control to the Lord. We are beholden to it. We live in a society of temperature-controlled buildings, appetite-control pills, and even control-top pantyhose. We want and seek control. Many of the women's movements direct women to take control of their lives, and though it's good to be organized in one's approach to life, you can never have complete control.

Princess Diana died while I was in the process of writing this book. She was a woman beloved of her fellow countrymen, and she acted with a servant's heart. People of all ages admired and respected her. I, too, felt touched by her death. But not because of the work she had done, or even because we are the same age and we both have two children. What hit me hard was the fact that she had no control over her death. *Well, of course not,* you say, *none of us have any control over our death.* But the reason Diana's death struck me so squarely was because Peter and I were planning on traveling to Spain about a month after she died. When she passed away, I suddenly felt very vulnerable to the unknown, particularly knowing I'd be far away from home. I wasn't afraid of dying—I have complete confidence in where I am going—but I did feel afraid of abandoning my children. Even now, nobody *knows* them as I do, nobody knows how to read their needs like I do, nobody knows how to comfort or admonish them as I do. In thinking about traveling to Spain, the fear of leaving my children and losing control over their growing-up years terrified me. Diana's death served to remind me how out of control my life is, every minute of every day.

Holding control of your life is a form of bondage. God can't work against the confines of your tight grip. For Him, it's like trying to take a piece of candy from a two-year-old. The more He tries to pry your fingers open, the more you stomp your feet, flail your arms, and fight.

My struggle with control or, rather, allowing the Lord to take it, used to be a constant in my life. Peter travels frequently on business. Interstate and internationally. For many years every time Peter went away I grieved. I feared losing him. It's as if I had to prepare myself each time he left for the possibility that he might not come back. How exhausting this became! I carried a coat of sadness over my arm—just waiting to put it on. I resolutely prepared to shrug my arms and shoulders into it whenever the need might arise. But it was an awfully heavy coat. It burdened me, it made my arms ache.

I gradually learned that as I walk with the Lord I can hand Him this coat of fear, sadness, grief, and, yes, control. He'll hang on to it for me. There is really no sense in dragging it around with me all the time. I've found that my hands and arms can accomplish so much more when I don't have that coat draped over my arms— when I relinquish control to the Lord.

Losing control to the Lord is just that—it's a loss. There is a grieving process that goes along with passing control to God. First there is the stranglehold of denial: "No, no, Lord. I don't think I can trust You with me!" (How ridiculous, He *made* me!) Then hot in-dignation brings bargaining: "Lord, really, can't You just give me back a thread of control?" (No, He can't. I can't be trusted with my life.)

Like the child with a piece of candy, I had such a firm grip on control that it was imprinted on my hand. I reminded myself during my preparations to leave for Spain that I had to peel away my fingers to release my grip on my life and that of my family. Then an exciting thing happened. A peace that indeed surpassed all understanding, because it was not born of my humanness, filled my heart and mind. I felt I could claim Psalm 121:7–8 with confidence: "The Lord will keep you from all harm—he will watch over your life; the Lord will watch over your coming and going both now and forevermore."

It's important to note God doesn't promise that no *bodily* harm will come to us. Of course we will get sick, and there will continue to be disease and tragedy in our worlds. Through those experiences, we will be drawn closer to Him. What He does promise is to protect our *souls*. Our salvation rests secure in Him, and with that assurance, we have permanent hope.

With this confidence, we'll find that we don't need to keep a wary vigil over our own lives or those of our family. Losing control to God and His timing is gaining freedom. The wait for Him to act no longer seems like a wait at all because we have handed Him our time clocks. Charles Swindoll says it this way: "When I keep my hands out of things, His will is accomplished, His name is exalted, and His glory magnified."[1]

WAITING ON THE LORD

Is waiting *on* the Lord the same as waiting *for* the Lord? No. While we are watchfully waiting for the Lord to act, are we impatiently tapping our feet? Probably yes, some of the time, but, more importantly, do we continue serving God or do we stop all activity to "wait" for Him? We can't literally sit motionless on our couches and wait—even though this book is about leading a spiritually tranquil life. In our stillness and our deepening desire to *know* God, we must continue to live for the Lord. Hence, even in our wait for the Lord to answer prayers or to act, we must continue to serve Him or to wait *on* Him. Even while we wait, there is a need to stay focused on Him, not on what we're waiting for.

SERVING THE LORD

When I think of waiting on the Lord, looking to what He needs us to do, I can't help but think of Mary and Martha. In Luke 10:38–42, Martha's gifts of hospitality and service propelled her to prepare food and lodging for Jesus and the disciples. She thought her preparations showed the Lord her respect, love, and devotion. Mary, on the other hand, motivated by her gifts of discernment and wisdom, felt she was serving her Master by giving Him her undivided attention. The Lord said Mary had chosen "what is better." Wholehearted devotion. She had chosen to be still (those two little words again) before the Lord. Mary served in stillness—where her gifts were best demonstrated. Martha served in action—where her gifts were best used.

Psalm 100:2 reminds us to "[serve] the Lord with gladness"; Galatians 5:13 says, "serve one another in love"; and Colossians 3:24 confirms, "It is the Lord Christ you are serving." But it seems lately that the concept of serving Christ and others is slowly losing its appeal. It doesn't seem fashionable in today's "serving number one" society. I find it humorous but a sad indicator of our self-centered times that the columnist "Dear Abby" sometimes prints accounts of "random acts of kindness." Why are they random acts and why are we so surprised when they happen? Because we have become hopelessly self-centered, and if an action isn't going to benefit us in some significant way we can't be bothered with it. We've become too self-absorbed to develop a servant's heart.

Traditionally, a servant knew what his master needed before the master even thought of it. A good servant anticipated and acted with very little direction from his or her employer. Servants were intelligent, perceptive, discerning, and above all, unobtrusive. They didn't call attention to their usefulness or skills; they didn't ask for recognition; they went about their tasks with confidence.

This perception and discernment are what we, as tranquil Christian women, can develop. When you watch for opportunities to serve Christ through serving others, you'll be amazed by how often those moments present themselves. The acts are done with a humble, quiet intent because the purpose is to bless someone by surprise. The result is that you've blessed the Creator in the process, because through Christ's love you viewed them as worthy of your time. I'm talking about simple acts here. Though comprehensive, unselfish events may occur, too, it's the frequent small acts that speak of a true servant's heart: holding the door for an elderly person; letting a young mother with small children in line ahead of you at the check-out counter; helping a neighbor with yard work without being asked; taking food to the home of a chronically ill person; saying an internal prayer for a harassed waitress or clerk; offering spontaneous words of appreciation; these all speak of serving others with Christ's love.

Second Corinthians 9:12–13 gives the twofold purpose of serving Christ through others:

> This service that you perform is not only supplying the needs of God's people but it is also overflowing in many expressions of thanks to God. Because of the service by which you have proved yourselves, men will praise God for the obedience that accompanies your confession of the gospel of Christ, and for your generosity in sharing with them and with everyone else.

Each act of service is a form of obedience to Christ. We serve Him when we serve others.

SUBMITTING TO THE LORD

While God is still holding us at His red light and cautioning us to watchfully wait, He is also reminding us that true stillness of the spirit comes with submission to Him. Job 22:21 says, "Submit to God and be at peace with him." Job, in his emotional and physical pain, is the epitome of staying faithful to God during extreme life circumstances. Here was a man who had every right not to feel peaceful about submitting to God. He could have grudgingly said, "Well, God, I will submit to you, but I'm not going to have a very good attitude about it." No, out of Job's own mouth it was affirmed that true submission to God produces peace.

This verse is such a great addendum to "Be still, and know that I am God." Job's words also express a sincere, willing surrender that only a heart at peace can produce. Once again, it is allowing God to be God and not fighting Him for His job.

A few pages ago I talked about my fear of leaving my children for a trip to Spain with my husband. It was only in complete submission to the Lord and to my husband that I was able to complete the trip. No, Peter didn't force me to go, but he had asked me a number of times to go, and I had always said no. I knew it was important for him and his business to show my support. But even more than that, going with Peter was an act of submission to God. It was relinquishing control and submitting to the authority of God. In submitting to God's will and His divine purpose for my life and that of my family, I found what Job was talking about. I stopped fretting. I stopped worrying. I became peaceful with God.

Submissiveness is born of Christian humility. I can see myself, in my mind's eye, bowed low before the Lord, not because He has forced me to my knees in feigned compliance, but because I desire to be in His shadow. Because I want, above all else, to be humble, still, peaceful, and respectful in His presence. I want to physically, emotionally, and spiritually submit to Him. In my submissive repose, I want to wait *on* the Lord, wait *for* the Lord, and wait *with* the Lord—with a servant's heart.

Jesus himself submitted to God when He was faced with death. In the Garden of Gethsemane, Jesus asked that the cup of death, the cup of excruciating pain and humility, be removed. Not once but three times He fell to His knees in emotional and spiritual anguish. But all three times God is silent in these passages, as if the silence itself is saying, "Submit, submit, submit." What an extreme and pro-found example of submission.

BEING GUARDED

In the same passages about Gethsemane from Matthew 26:36–46, Jesus asked His disciples to keep watch with Him. I have no doubt their hearts were willing to stay up all night with their Lord, but they were humans in need of physical sleep. He didn't even bother to wake them the second time He found them sleeping. Why did they sleep? Because Jesus had to keep watch alone and resolve once and for all His commitment to go to the Cross and fulfill the Father's will. This was God's plan. No one could make it easier; no one could take away or lessen the impact of what was about to hap-pen. Even if the disciples had been awake, they couldn't have changed the scene or saved Him from His betrayer.

During those restless hours, Jesus took the responsibility of guardianship for our lives squarely on His back. This He would carry to the Cross, along with our sins. In the wake of Christ's death, the disciples were no longer needed to stand watch with Christ; now He would permanently stand watch over us.

GUARDING YOUR HEART

Christ became our guardian, our intermediary. Because of His death, He stands between us and the black hole of our sin. It's quite a stretch. The breadth and width of our sin is so wide, He is figu-ratively pulled in four directions. But He'll stand in this gap for us for all eternity. We do have a choice and responsibility to attempt to close the gap—by guarding our own hearts, by accepting His promise to keep us in the hour of temptation and deliver us from evil.

In a state of unconfessed sin, we can't be still before God. The guilt of sin will force us to try to cover up, erase, delete, and recover ground we've already passed over once. It is a useless waste of spiritual energy. But we can take protective action in advance by confessing our sins, accepting His forgiveness, and asking Him to erect a hedge of protection around us so that we can be still before Him.

We can reinforce the hedge by arming ourselves with the truth, memorizing Scripture, avoiding situations that could lead to temptation, and spending time daily with Him. These are all building blocks to keep ourselves safe within the hedge of His protection and care.

Ephesians 6:14–17 reminds us of the availability of God's hedge of protection when we put on the "full armor of God":

> Stand firm then, with the belt of truth buckled around your waist, with the breastplate of righteousness in place, and with your feet fitted with the readiness that comes from the gospel of peace. In addition to this, take up the shield of faith, with which you can extinguish all the flaming arrows of the evil one. Take the helmet of salvation and the sword of the Spirit, which is the word of God.

I love the imagery in this passage! We are in a field of battle where the Enemy's darts would wound us, but the Lord's armor is solid enough to protect us.

Another promise, the one that I felt profoundly when I relinquished control to the Lord, is in Philippians 4:7: "And the peace of God, which transcends all understanding, will guard your hearts and your minds in Christ Jesus."

SETTING BOUNDARIES

The walls of protection around us are both barriers and boundaries. The barriers keep evil out, and the boundaries keep us in.

A couple of years ago I bought Peter an eighteen-month-old black-lab-mix puppy from the Humane Society. She was an absolute love, adoring anyone around her. But that was just the problem—she had no doggy discernment as to whom she belonged. Because she was young and hadn't lived with us for very long, she hadn't developed an undivided loyalty yet. Tail wagging, tongue lolling, she followed anyone walking by on the road. A couple of times we found her several miles from home. Naughty dog. But we realized she was only doing what she had done all her young life. Wandering. Which is why she ended up at the Humane Society. The question we needed to answer was, how could we communicate to her that this was unacceptable and dangerous behavior? We live on a large farm; tying her up seemed a shame, plus she barked, and confining her to a pen defeated the purpose of having a dog. We settled on invisible fencing, which, when she wore a special collar, gave her a warning beep, followed by a small shock if she got too close to the boundary lines laid out for her. She learned to respect the boundary; she learned she was free to roam and play inside the lines. She seemed to stop fretting about what she could find beyond our home, and we stopped worrying about her getting lost. Within the boundary lines, she was safe and protected.

As with our wayward dog, when we agree to boundary lines we find ourselves to be truly free. When we've prayed for clear guidance and constructed the boundaries, there is no question where the lines are. There is safety and protection within them and uncertainty and danger without. We are happier and more secure within God's limits. Psalm 16:5–6 says, "You have made my lot secure. The boundary lines have fallen for me in pleasant places; surely I have a delightful inheritance." And Psalm 119:45, "I will walk about in freedom, for I have sought out your precepts."

Clear boundaries can also set you free from past bondages. Ropes and chains that have held you captive drop the moment you step within the Lord's protective boundary. Any bondage—fear, control, manipulation, lust, drink, abuse, gambling—can hold you in its grip against your will. This isn't the same stillness that God wants for us. The stillness of bondage is a trap, tearing at your flesh, breaking your bones, damaging your self-worth. (Look for more about bondages and guilt in chapter 8.)

Within God's protective boundaries, we are safe to rest, to be still, and to wait for the Lord.

Stillness in Action

While in a quiet place, reflect on a time when you were watchfully waiting for the Lord to answer a prayer or act in a particular situation. In a creative way, express to the Lord how you felt during the wait and how you felt when the wait was over. (Suggestions: draw or paint a picture, write a poem, gather mementos from your home, sing a song, find items from nature and arrange them in a collage.) Read Psalm 40:1–5 for a graphic before-and-after portrait that David wrote in response to the Lord's faithfulness.

MEMORY VERSE

"Yet the Lord longs to be gracious to you; he rises to show you compassion. For the Lord is a God of justice. Blessed are all who wait for him!"

ISAIAH 30:18

PART TWO

And Know

CHAPTER SIX

Wisdom

"Blessed is the man who finds wisdom,
the man who gains understanding."

PROVERBS 3 : 13

"O Lord, give me wisdom!"

My prayer, in itself confessing my lack of knowledge, gave me
the feeling I had an illuminating spotlight on my soul. I didn't know
what to do.

Peter and I were faced with the difficult and daunting decision
of where to send our nine-year-old Geneva to school. She had at-
tended a private Christian school through the third grade, but her
psychosomatic ailments forced us to take a serious look at the education she was receiving beyond academics. Headaches, tummy-
aches, and insomnia, all present during schooltimes and notably ab-
sent during school vacations throughout the third grade, forced us
into our collective prayer for wisdom and direction.

God had entrusted us with our daughter. We knew we were responsible to raise her in the "admonition of the Lord." But we didn't know which avenue would best accent her strengths, help her in her weaknesses, and most importantly, encourage her security and growth into a godly young woman. Which was the right choice: continued private education, where she was obviously struggling; public education, where we felt concern about ungodly influences; or home education, where we felt unqualified? When our children were born, we had no idea how much we would agonize over their education!

"Lord, you gave Geneva to us to raise to the best of our ability, but we don't know *how*! Wisdom, *please*!"

Our decision to educate Geneva at home came only as I asked for confirmation of that particular choice as being God's will. I didn't say, "Okay, Lord, we'll keep Geneva home for a year. Is that fine with you?" Knowing that the Lord's life plan and will for Geneva might well be beyond what I could comprehend, I simply asked for open and closed doors. Doors closed for other options until we were left with the one choice: home education. And I still dragged my feet. Her fourth-grade year and Jordan's first-grade year would be the first time in ten years that I would have seven uninterrupted hours to myself each school day. How I had longed for time of my own again! But as Peter and I felt more and more impressed with the knowledge that Geneva's well-being was reliant on her staying home for at least a year, I knew I'd have to put my desires aside for a while longer. I knew home education would be the most unselfish thing I had ever done, but I also felt that the Lord had given us clear direction and wisdom about the decision. He showed us what Geneva's needs were; He gave us confirming signs; and He granted Peter and I like-mindedness in our conclusions.

WHY DO WE NEED WISDOM TO BE STILL?

Any life-altering decision takes time to make. Prayer, reading, seeking wise counsel, and researching are all a part of any major decision. When we pray for wisdom, we are essentially seeking to determine the will of God. We're trying to see just a glimpse, just a thread of the mind of God. We want to know what God wants.

"Be still, *and know* that I am God."

It is only in stillness that we can truly know God. We talked about spiritual attention deficit disorder, where the person affected is in constant motion. How can we know God—know Him intimately, know His nature, know His will, know His mind, have His wisdom—if we don't first remain still long enough to understand what His mind and wisdom are? His wisdom is available to us for the asking. When we begin to understand His wisdom, we will catch a glimpse of who God is—of His undeniable trustworthiness. When we embrace the truth of His all-knowing mind and His complete faithfulness, we can rest and be at peace—letting God be God.

GOD'S WISDOM IS FROM THE BEGINNING

Proverbs 3:19–20 reads, "By wisdom the Lord laid the earth's foundations, by understanding he set the heavens in place; by his knowledge the deeps were divided, and the clouds let drop the dew." In 8:22, Wisdom is speaking in the first person: "The Lord brought me forth as the first of his works, before his deeds of old." And verse 27: "I was there when he set the heavens in place, when he marked out the horizon on the face of the deep."

Wisdom was there at the beginning of time. It was an essential ingredient before any other form could come to be. Wisdom is the basic defining characteristic of God. It was with wisdom that "In the beginning God created the heavens and the earth" (Genesis 1:1). God is wisdom. Wisdom is God. Wisdom is the be-all and end-all. God's wisdom is infinite and undefinable. Words can't express the magnitude and sheer infinity of the Lord's wisdom.

Yet Solomon wrote extensively about wisdom, its characteristics, how to get it, how to act in it, what it produces in our lives. Is the wisdom he was describing for mankind the same as God's wisdom? Yes and no.

God's wisdom is absolute knowledge. It is pure. It is truth. There is no question about its perfection—His wisdom is perfect. We cannot have this same depth of wisdom, because we are sinners. As a result of Eve's sin in having picked and tasted the fruit of the Tree of Knowledge, we will never be able to fully understand or grasp the profundity of God's knowledge or wisdom this side of heaven. We have to take it by faith that He knows more than we do! So in this sense, no, we don't have the same wisdom as God. But the good news is God has given us the spiritual capability to draw on some of His wisdom. We don't have the depth or purity or intensity of God's wisdom, but we have access to a portion by simple request. God answers with a taste of His wisdom—what we need to know for that time and place.

Tony Evans says in his book *Our God Is Awesome*, "Wisdom means the ability to take a divine, spiritual perspective and turn it into an earthly, functional application."[1]

HUMAN WISDOM

How many times have you prayed for wisdom concerning a pending decision or difficult circumstance? In my years of involvement in Bible studies and women's groups, I've heard women ask for wisdom countless times. But there were times when I felt dubious asking for wisdom. The prayer somehow seemed trite. What exactly was I asking for? The mind and knowledge of God himself? Who did I think I was? I felt as though I hadn't lived enough—or died enough—to ask for or claim wisdom for myself. In my early thirties, I felt too young and unqualified to pursue what may be considered "an old man's inheritance." I began to invest time in understanding and pursuing wisdom in my life. You can, too.

Wisdom is all-consuming counsel available for our Christian walk. We are instructed in Proverbs to seek wisdom with our whole beings:

[My daughter], if you accept my words and store up my commands within you, turning your ear to wisdom and applying your heart to understanding, and if you call out for insight and cry aloud for understanding, and if you look for it as for silver and search for it as for hidden treasure, then you will understand the fear of the Lord and find the knowledge of God. Proverbs 2:2–5.

These verses are incredible! Can't you just see someone scratching about in the earth, searching for the hidden treasure of wisdom? Or calling out from the mountaintop, waiting for an echoing reply? The intensity of the search that Solomon recommends here requires three of your five senses: turning your ear to listen, looking with your eyes, and searching with your tactile hands. This wisdom is so valuable it should take up a great deal of our days and lives seeking it!

But, once again, because of our attention deficit lives, we forget or become distracted by other things. We worry, we agonize, we speculate, we discuss, and we weigh the options. We need to remember to arm ourselves with wisdom *first*. We need to pray for increasing wisdom on a daily basis, not only when we are faced with a question. Having wisdom readily available at our fingertips helps to minimize our distracting anxieties.

WHAT IS WISDOM?

Let me give you an example of wisdom in action.

I have a dear college-age friend. During her first year of college, she was confronted with a number of potentially character-damaging situations. Each day she prayed for the Lord's wisdom on how to deal with them in a godly way. There was a young man she was interested in getting to know better. He was handsome, godly, and seemed to be a hard worker—all traits she felt marked a man as potential dating material. One weekend she and a group of friends were invited to his home for pizza and a movie. She planned to go, knowing it would be an excellent opportunity to get to know him in a group setting.

But then the young woman who had offered to drive the group to his apartment suggested they stop first for a drink at the local pub. My friend hedged. She *really* wanted to get to know this guy, but she didn't want to drink. What to do? Go to the pub, have tea, then arrive at his apartment with her possibly tipsy friends? Would it compromise her personal convictions to be with a group that was drinking? Would it reflect poorly on her to the young man even if she hadn't been drinking? She spent a day and a half trying to decide what to do. Finally, after private prayer, she came to the conclusion that even if it meant losing out on getting to know the young man to whom she felt attracted, it wasn't worth compromising her standards to be with people who might be under the influence of alcohol. She wasn't condemning what they were doing; she just wanted to get to know the young man under pure, ungiddy circumstances.

That's wisdom. She put aside her wants—a desire to get to know the young man—and asked God what would be the wisest choice. The Lord showed her that if this man was someone He wanted to bring into her life, other opportunities would transpire for them to get to know each other. Her strength of character and resolve were evidence of the wisdom she prayed for every day. She took Proverbs 2:10 to task: "For wisdom will enter your heart, and knowledge will be pleasant to your soul. Discretion will protect you, and understanding will guard you."

Wisdom, in human terms, is finely tuned spiritual knowledge. It is precise. Wisdom is a pinpoint of light that can illuminate any situation—like a struck match touching a candlewick, it flares to life, lighting up a dark corner.

Wisdom is the very foundation of our spiritual lives. The minute we ask Jesus into our hearts to be Lord and Savior of our lives, a seed of wisdom takes root in our soul. It grows as our relationship with the Lord grows. And it never stops. We can never have too much wisdom, nor can we ever use it all up. It is always there for us to draw upon.

It is out of this foundational wisdom that our other gifts are manifested. Wisdom is the entirety of all the spiritual gifts rolled into one. Wisdom gives us the knowledge and capability to use our spiritual gifts appropriately and effectively. All the other gifts are filtered first through wisdom. Proverbs 8:12 says, "I, wisdom, dwell together with prudence; I possess knowledge and discretion." When you have gained even an ounce of wisdom in your life, you have the ability to know when, where, how, and why to use the gifts God has given you, because with each gift is a portion of wisdom. Praying for wisdom is praying for opportunities to use the innate gifts God has entrusted to you. When we pray for wisdom, God's reply will be, "I have given you unique gifts, skills, and abilities. My wisdom is available to you through them."

When Peter and I prayed for wisdom to know what the best schooling solution was for Geneva, both of us used our gifts to help determine God's will. My discernment was put to the test first, deciphering what Geneva's needs were, then determining where they could be met. Peter's exhortation encouraged and nurtured both Geneva and me anytime we felt discouraged and helped to keep us on track. Wisdom was given to us through the use of our other gifts.

WHO IS WISDOM?

"Who?" Isn't wisdom a trait, a gift, a characteristic? It is a gift, but it is also so powerful and unique that when Solomon wrote about gaining wisdom he had to give it a persona.

Proverbs 8 is written in the first person, Wisdom speaking. Wisdom has such a strong, individual identity that it is even assigned the female gender. Starting out with, "Does not wisdom call out? Does not understanding raise her voice?" And then in the second verse: "Where the paths meet, she takes her stand," and in verses 3 and 4: "She cries aloud: 'To you, O men, I call out; I raise my voice to all mankind.'" And then further on, in verse 23, "'I was appointed from eternity, from the beginning, before the world began.'" Verses 29–30: "'. . . when he marked out the foundations of the earth. Then I was the craftsman at his side.'" Chapter 9:1–2 reads, "Wisdom has built her house; she has hewn out its seven pillars. . . . She has also set her table." This wisdom Solomon wrote about is distinctly *feminine*. Wisdom in these verses is almost like the bride of the Lord. She helped to create the house of the Lord, the world. She is God's right hand, she's creative, she's hospitable, and she's precious. Wisdom is God's helpmate and homemaker.

With Wisdom there is a coming together of two parts. First is this feminine persona as defined by Solomon, and second is the wisdom of God—the sieve through which the gifts He's given us come. Because Solomon so wisely gave us this word picture of wisdom as a person, we are able to relate to her on a female level and incorporate her as part of our lives. It is the same wisdom that was with God when He created the universe, only it is clothed in human terms.

It is a simultaneously humbling and exciting thought that the wisdom from the beginning of time is available to us! Proverbs 3:7, though, suggests a word of caution: "Do not be wise in your own eyes." But as you study and begin to understand the magnitude of God's wisdom and how it is available to us, you become more humble, not proud! This is because we begin to see just how finite we are. A truly wise person knows she can never be wise enough. The wiser we get, the more we know what we don't know. James 3:13 confirms this: "Who is wise and understanding among you? Let him show it by his good life, by deeds done in the humility that comes from wisdom." The wiser you get, the more humbled you are! And the more humbled you are, the freer you will be to stay still in God's wisdom, because there is nothing else but God's wisdom, and all we have to do is be still and let His wisdom work through us and for our benefit.

WHERE IS WISDOM?

The entirety of Proverbs was written as a guide to gaining wisdom. Chapter 1 begins:

> The proverbs of Solomon son of David, king of Israel: for attaining wisdom and discipline; for understanding words of insight; for acquiring a disciplined and prudent life, doing what is right and just and fair; for giving prudence to the simple, knowledge and discretion to the young—let the wise listen and add to their learning, and let the discerning get guidance.

When I began to seek to understand the significance of wisdom and thereby gain an ounce of it, I went through the book of Proverbs day by day. I did this for several months (have you heard the adage "a Proverb a day keeps the devil away"?). I underlined every reference to wisdom in red and paraphrased the meanings of various verses in my journal. I underlined references about knowledge in black and deciphered connections between wisdom and knowledge. Two of the many conclusions I came to, as I've already shared, were that wisdom began with God at the creation of the world, and that it is available to us in measures throughout our life. And, as I related from Proverbs 2, it should be one of the main focuses of our spiritual walk—a quest for wisdom. Initially I thought this might be a bit presumptuous—praying for God's wisdom—but I realized the more I understood about wisdom, and the deeper the relationship I developed with the Lord, that it likely would be through the quest itself that wisdom would be revealed. I will never "feel" wise enough—if I did, I wouldn't need the Lord. Instead, I learned that gaining wisdom is an ongoing daily process that will never be exhausted.

WHAT IS TO BE GAINED FROM WISDOM?

There is more to be gained from the acquisition of wisdom than Wisdom itself. A number of promises are offered throughout Proverbs for those who would gain wisdom. Chapter 24:14 says, "Know also that wisdom is sweet to your soul; if you find it, there is a future hope for you, and your hope will not be cut off." And 14:24: "The wealth of the wise is their crown." The benefit here is a life-giving treasure.

Chapter 2:12–16 tells us that wisdom will save us from a number of ills, including the deceitfulness of others, perverseness, personal deviousness, adultery, etc. Wisdom, again, is the illuminating light that gives us a sharp distinction between right and wrong. Wisdom's discernment allows us to see with certain clarity what is not godly. Wisdom stands guard over our spiritual lives.

The power of wisdom is found in Proverbs 8:12–21. In paraphrase, wisdom offers counsel and sound judgment, sanctions rulers to rule, and gives a harvest of riches. In 3:13–18 it discusses the blessings of gaining wisdom. Paraphrased, it is valuable, an investment against the future, dear to the heart, full of life-giving quiet, and provides secure living. This wisdom really is worth seeking!

The value and merit of wisdom is best summed up in 4:5–7:

> Get wisdom, get understanding; do not forget my words or swerve from them. Do not forsake wisdom, and she will protect you; love her, and she will watch over you. Wisdom is supreme; therefore get wisdom. Though it cost all you have, get understanding.

With such a direct, specific admonition, how can we possibly ignore the advice of Solomon? Gaining wisdom is like an insurance policy on your soul. Proverbs 19:8: "He who gets wisdom loves his own soul."

WHO CAN RECEIVE WISDOM?

You can! As I learned, it is not an old man's inheritance, granted only on the cusp of death. And though older people are usually wiser than younger people, simply because they have experienced more life, young people should seek wisdom wholeheartedly. That's exactly why Solomon wrote the Proverbs—he didn't think we, young or old, should wait for wisdom to find us. Rather, we need to earnestly seek it. When we recognize the magnitude and consequence of having God's wisdom permeate our lives, when we are no longer reliant on our own wisdom or knowledge, imagine how much more effective we will become. When we let go of our own knowledge and actively pursue God's wisdom, we *become still* to our humanness and, once again, allow God to be God through us.

WISDOM IN YOUR GIFTEDNESS

Wisdom gives you the authority to use your gifts and the knowledge as to when and how to use them. Wisdom also gives you discrimination, offering guidelines for practical use of your gifts. Within the boundaries of wisdom, you can use your God-given gifts with energy and joy. Wisdom protects you from overuse of your gifts; it prevents burnout, fatigue, and feelings of being taken advantage of.

Wisdom reminds me of a competitive sports game (despite not being a very big fan of professional competitive sports). Wisdom is always present, ready to play the ball that has been passed its way. Wisdom is on offense, looking for opportunities to move, run, target the goal, and make a score. Wisdom observes, listens, reads the situation around you, and moves in to connect with the action.

Wisdom doesn't react, but responds. You respond to what you see with your unique gifts to serve the situation for the Lord. If your response is simply a reaction, you haven't allowed Wisdom to give you the details, or invited Wisdom to give you a flash of discernment to decipher the needs of the moment. People who *react* to situations are the ones who end up feeling tired, used, and unappreciated. People who *respond* to situations, using their gifts, feel blessed and utilized as an instrument of the Lord. Let me give you a few examples.

Both Peter and I have the gift of giving. If given the opportunity, I could easily drain our bank account giving to worthy Christian causes. Peter is also a generous encourager. He is a cheerleader; generous in offering support, kind words, pats on the back, and compliments such as "You did a great job!" But both of our generous natures can get us into trouble, too.

We have a single friend who has needed money in the past. We had given him small amounts here and there because we saw his need, felt able to help, and felt led to give to him. He came to us once more, not directly asking for money, but implying things were tough, bills needed to be paid, and he couldn't find enough work to meet his needs. My first inclination was to once more get out the checkbook. But then I stopped for a minute. I realized I was simply reacting to his need, not responding in a way that would ultimately help him. I decided to look at his situation a little more objectively. I prayed for the best way to help him; I asked for wisdom in using my gift of generosity. As Peter and I talked, we both came to the conclusion that it was time for this man to help himself. In Alcoholics Anonymous, the person who buys the alcohol for an alcoholic is termed an "enabler," because he is enabling the alcoholic to continue to drink. We were in a position to enable this young man toward becoming somewhat helpless. We wanted to change that pattern. We made a few phone calls and located a part-time job that would help to meet his financial needs. At first, he seemed a little disappointed. Money straight from our pockets would have been a lot easier. But we knew we couldn't allow him to become dependent on us and unable to do for himself. Our generosity, tempered with wisdom, in this case meant *not* giving him money.

I am also blessed with the spiritual gift of mercy, though sometimes this can feel like a heavy, heavy burden. My mercy shows up the most in my compassion for animals. I find it indicative of God's love for His entire creation that He chose to save only eight human beings from the Flood and two of every animal He had created. Reading through the Bible produces many accounts of the value of animals in God's eyes. My deep compassion for "the beasts of the field" has earned me the nickname "The Keeper of the Animals." Indeed, I see myself as a true daughter of Noah—understanding animals' nature and needs.

Of course the problem with this is I would take in every stray, every forlorn, every homeless, every abused animal that crossed my path. Between my generosity and concern for animal welfare, I could easily be eaten out of house and home! Fortunately, temperance, frequently in the form of my husband, steps in to prevent this gift from going too far.

I also know that wisdom has been present in each acquisition of a new animal. (We currently have two dogs, three cats, and four horses.) When I picked out a dog from the Humane Society for Peter's birthday (the dog that kept running away), I remember standing before a row of caged dogs, each set of imploring eyes capturing mine. I would have taken every one home, but Wisdom overruled my mercy, and I settled on our dog who came to be known as Gibraltar because I felt God's hand and whisper of affirmation each time I looked at her. She has turned out to be absolutely the best dog for our family and home. In hindsight, I think the Lord had her in mind for us, because other potential owners might not have had the patience needed to train this dog. He knew I would.

As a thought of conjecture, say I had taken every dog home with me. Would I have been able to give each one the attention, training, affection, and food it needed? No! "Well, that's common sense," you say. Of course it is! But in this perhaps overly simplistic story, I want you to see how, sometimes, we all could get dragged in by a pretty face or a point of need and end up in over our heads. All in the name of using our gifts!

Wisdom prevents all that. Wisdom knows the cutoff point. Wisdom knows where enough is enough. Wisdom knows when you are tempted to wade in over your head. Wisdom is the voice that tells you, "Don't take another step or you'll find yourself in very deep water."

When have you gone too far in using one of your gifts? Perhaps in using your gift of hospitality, you agreed to host a church supper . . . for two hundred. Or, because of your gift of service, you agreed to take a whole Saturday away from your family to help move an acquaintance. Or, because of your gift of administration, you agreed to be the Sunday school superintendent, even though you work forty hours a week outside your home. When faced with tasks that use our gifts, our immediate *reaction* is to jump in because we think, "I know how to do this! I can help!" (Plus, it feels good to be needed.) But wisdom must be allowed to *respond* to the point of need first, before your gift takes over.

When wisdom is allowed the first position in your offensive line, you will really be useful to the Lord. You will no longer be stretched to the breaking point; you will no longer feel like you're missing the plays because of spiritual ADD. With wisdom in full play with you, you can watchfully be still, waiting for the Lord to pass you the ball He has in mind for you to play.

Stillness in Action

Make a commitment to read one Proverb a day for six months. Start today—why not now? Also mark off a separate section in your journal, or buy a spiral notebook for note-taking. As I did, mark every reference to wisdom in Proverbs with a colored pen or highlighter. Paraphrase what it means to you in your notebook. Make notes about how you can apply certain references to your life about gaining wisdom. As wisdom grows in your heart, I

know the Lord will give you occasion to put it to the test.
Pray for such opportunities!

MEMORY VERSE

**"For wisdom will enter your heart, and knowledge will be
pleasant to your soul. Discretion will protect you,
and understanding will guard you."**
(To give this verse a very personal meaning, change the pronouns
to "me" and "my.")

PROVERBS 2:10–11

CHAPTER SEVEN

Head Knowledge

"He has made everything beautiful in its time.
He has also set eternity in the hearts of men;
yet they cannot fathom what God has done
from beginning to end."

ECCLESIASTES 3:11

Growing up, I spent a lot of time at my grandparents'
home, Sweetwood Farm. My grandfather (the one I wrote of in
chapter 3) and grandmother always welcomed me with open arms.
Innately knowing what a privilege it was to have them in my life, I
always acted on my best behavior whenever I visited them. A particularly special honor was when I or one of my two older sisters
was asked to spend the night at Sweetwood. I knew pampering, a
special meal, undivided attention, and a quiet room to myself were
guaranteed with this offer.

As a very young child, I can remember sitting at their dining
room table, my shoulders barely reaching the top of it. My grandfather would say, "I have just the solution for you!" Then he'd pull
out the biggest dictionary I have ever seen, before or since. It must

have been close to six or seven inches deep. He'd lift me off the chair, place the dictionary on the seat, then plunk me on top of the giant book. With the heavy binder under my bottom, I could see over the table, reach my food without spilling, and carry on a grown-up conversation while eye to eye with my grandparents. Pompere would frequently comment about the book upon which I sat as being one of the most important books I could ever avail myself of. "You can never know enough, you can never stop learning," he would instruct. Being a teacher, his own thirst for knowledge and a desire to pass that passion on to his grandchildren were felt by each one of us. To him, the answer to every one of life's ills could be corrected with knowledge. He was a lifetime scholar and a follower of "The More You Know" campaign before it was fashionable.

I had a great respect and admiration for my grandfather, and I still do. He taught me so many lessons about "finding answers" and recognizing life lessons from the world around me (he was an avid gardener in his retirement years). I owe a great deal to him, recognizing how he shaped my view of learning.

However, even as a young child, I sensed that to my grandfather knowledge meant more than knowing the answers. It meant power, it meant control. It meant always being on top, always being prepared with answers. It sometimes seemed like he had a fear of being caught off guard, of being unprepared for a battle of the wits. There were times when I felt a little uneasy, knowing I likely couldn't live up to his expectations of how much I should be learning and how much I should know. I felt afraid of disappointing him during the years when I had less than an enthusiastic approach to my schoolwork. Though I never doubted he loved me and was proud of me, during my teen years I know he felt skeptical of the depth of my education. When I graduated from nursing school, I remember him saying, "Bravo! We couldn't be happier for you!" Then in the next breath he said, "You could be a doctor, you know."

I knew I could, too, I just didn't want to go to school anymore!

FORMING MY OWN OPINIONS

As my walk with the Lord took a definitive path of its own, I
found that I needed to clarify just how I felt about education.
Though I valued my grandfather's opinion, I needed to find my own
definition. Is education—head knowledge—the be-all and end-all?
Should we, as Christians, be pursuing it with our whole lives? Is the
pursuit of head knowledge in line with "being still" before the Lord?
I have developed my own educational philosophy, which, along with
establishing learning principles for home schooling, has helped me
to put boundaries on the restless nature of the pursuit of knowledge:
Education is what you make of it. Basically, education is as much or
as little as you want to put into the effort of the resources you are
given. For example, you can take a classic piece of literature, say,
Moby Dick, and learn/teach a dozen different concepts from it:
grammar, punctuation, calculations, decision-making, character
traits, geography, history, cultures, etc. And all it's cost you is the
price of the book (better yet, borrow it from the library).

Let me give you another example. Between the first college I at-
tended and the one where I received my nursing degree, I worked
for six months as a nurse's aide, then traveled to Europe on a college-
sponsored eight-week study of the Reformation. It cost several
thousand dollars, and I earned only three history credits for it. By
comparison, I could have spent about the same amount of money
for a semester at an Ivy League college and undertaken some book
knowledge. But which choice gave me unique, hands-on lessons?
The traveling, of course. What I learned on that trip could never
have been replicated in a classroom. (Not to mention the fact I met
Peter on that trip.) The lessons I learned on my European journey
have lasted me a lifetime. Yet I can barely remember the specific
content of my elective nursing school classes. Again, education is
what you make of it.

No, I don't have a haphazard, casual approach to education, but
I do have a concern for those who make a career out of pursuing

higher education: what exactly are career students after?

Educational knowledge, or human knowledge, can have its traps. That's not to say we shouldn't learn what we need to know to live godly, productive lives—lives by which we can minister with our gifts and raise up our children in the admonition of the Lord. But the all-out, no-holds-barred pursuit of knowledge has become a god to some students. In essence, what they are searching for is absolute truth. Absolute, pure knowledge.

Yes, it is good to stretch ourselves, to know where to look for answers, to hold well-informed conversations, to understand the world around us, and to formulate researched opinions. But when the quest for these attributes takes the place of the one and only Truth, we've removed our focus from God himself.

The Shorter Catechism, compiled and written by G. I. Williamson, confronts the pursuit of knowledge this way: "Man, of himself, can not really come to the knowledge of the truth. The more a man learns by his own effort (by the unaided power of his own mind), the more he faces the unknown. Just as a balloon, when it is blown up, expands in every direction, so does man's learning bring him face-to-face with the endless mystery of the wonderful works of God."[1] We can't be content in God being God if our attention is directed toward the exclusivity of knowledge. We weren't meant to know all the answers. Actually, the quest for head knowledge has a very scary root.

IT'S ALL EVE'S FAULT!

The very core of original sin was Eve's desire for head knowledge and to be as wise as God. When the serpent slyly asked Eve about God's command to not eat the fruit of a certain tree in the middle of the garden, he sneered at her reply that she and Adam were not allowed to eat from it. He scoffed, " 'You will not surely die. . . . For God knows that when you eat of it your eyes will be opened, and you will be like God, knowing good and evil.' When the woman saw that the fruit of the tree was good for food and pleasing to the eye, and also desirable for gaining wisdom, she took some and ate it" (Genesis 3:4–6).

I often wonder, *What in heaven's name was Eve thinking?* How could she want more than what had been already given to her? She couldn't have even known there was more to be had. Eden was all she had known. What did she possibly have to be discontent about? But it's important to note that it wasn't her own inner dissatisfaction that caused her to reach for the forbidden fruit. It was the serpent who led her to wonder, *Maybe there's more to Eden.* The serpent also planted doubt in Eve's mind about her self-esteem, her worthiness, and her intellect. Perhaps she thought, *Maybe it would be good to have God's wisdom; to know everything without having to learn it. After all, I have no instruction guide about how to garden, how to be a wife, or how to take care of these animals. A bit of God's knowledge would give me everything I need to know.* It didn't take much convincing from the serpent after that. Eve even invited Adam to eat. How unselfish of her to share her newfound independence and rebellion with Adam!

Do you see how the very root of Eve's sin was a lust for knowledge, to have the mind of *God* himself? That root is still evident in some today. It's a double-forked root: a quest for complete knowledge and a general dissatisfaction with life's circumstances.

DISSATISFACTION

Peter and I created our farm from scratch. When we bought our home, forests covered the once grassy fields—it has taken us twelve years to reclaim those fields bit by bit. One of our first undertakings was to build a barn in one of the few clearings. Instead of a quaint old farmhouse, we live in a renovated summer cottage. Again, it took twelve years of sweat, labor, and money.

I try to live by the adage that says a woman has the ability to make a house into a home. I like our home and property to be attractive. However, the elderly couple from whom we bought the land and cottage had what I viewed as an eclectic landscaping plan. Thrown-together stone walls, patches of day lilies in the middle of the lawn, and an evergreen tree that scratched the entryway door each time it opened. There were also two enormous rhododendron bushes clinging to the edge of a slope beyond our backyard.

I liked those huge rhododendron bushes. I loved the bright, full, pinkish-purple blossoms in the spring. I just didn't like where the bushes were located. It seemed an odd spot to me, sort of an over-the-edge afterthought. I decided that I would move them closer to the house and start my own landscaping. I ambitiously went to work with a spade shovel. After a very short time I hit a root. No problem, I'd work around it and loosen it. I don't know if you have ever tried to pull up a rhododendron bush, but take my advice: Don't. Those bushes were so firmly entrenched in the ground, there was no way my little spade shovel would be able to dig the sinewy roots out. I re-covered the tough roots with dirt, walked away, and learned to admire the bushes from a distance.

A number of years later I was talking with a friend of mine who is a landscape artist. When I told him about my attempt to move the rhododendron bush, he laughed. "You can't move those without a backhoe and tractor!" he hooted. Well, *now* I know that. Apparently the root of a rhododendron is actually a ball with tough, knotted roots spidering off from it. When a rhododendron decides to take root, nobody is going to move it!

Now those bushes, visible from the window next to my kitchen table, frequently serve to remind me of the depth of the roots of dissatisfaction that were in my life. Perhaps you, too, have found dissatisfaction so entrenched in your life that it's hard to remove it— that is because it is the very same root that has spidered through the generations from Eve and Adam.

What are the areas of dissatisfaction in your life? Perhaps it's discontentment with how you look, or where you live, or about the choices your children are making, or your job, or your mate. There's so much to be discontent with! In my own life, my dissatisfaction comes through in how I feel about myself. I set lofty goals, write long "to do" lists, and mark "must complete" notes on my calendar. I inevitably set myself up for feelings of failure! There are never enough hours in the day to accomplish what I sometimes think I have time for. Then I get mad at myself. I even get snippy with my family when it's not their fault that *I* overscheduled! Dissatisfaction hangs over me in a dark cloud, dripping on everyone around me.

But, as I've learned to be still in the Lord, somehow my discontentment evaporates. I love the title of the book *Don't Sweat the Small Stuff . . . and It's All Small Stuff* by Dr. Richard Carlson. Though it's not necessarily a Christian book, the title is a great maxim. Viewing our world from under God's protective wing, it seems everything else pales and becomes little. All the "stuff" in my life (frequently there at the request of my own hands) seems inconsequential when I remember my desired "be still" demeanor, when I remember that God is a God of complete contentment.

There can be no discontentment with the almighty God. Looking again at the Twenty-third Psalm and David's deep understanding of God's profound sufficiency, we can't help but be satisfied with the knowledge that God will watch over our every need. He will anticipate each of our physical, emotional, and spiritual needs before we even know of them. Discontentment has no place in Psalm 23. Just as Eden could have been a place of complete contentment for Eve, we, as the sheep of God's holy flock, have the same opportunity to know complete contentment if we stay within the confines of His pasture. But just as Eve discovered, if we sidestep God's simple rules, we will find ourselves "cast out."

Toward the end of each calendar year I look back over my journal entries from the preceding year. It gives me confidence and proof that I'm increasing my spiritual reserves. It reminds me of lessons learned from times when I wandered off for a bit, thinking I was headed for greener pastures, when in reality I'd been ambling toward a pit. Each written journal entry has shown me God's impeccable timing in bringing me back to His fold. And these little blips seemed to have come further and further apart. That's gratifying. I've felt even more encouraged as several times I've come across a theme that convinced me I was indeed practicing stillness in my life. The entries went something like this:

> Lord, at this moment I love my life. I love that the opportunities You have given me to be a wife, mother, homemaker, writer, and rider give me complete fulfillment. I love my lack of restlessness. I love my contentedness. I love that my family allows me to act on my convictions of stillness. I love that You've brought me through feelings of discontent, inadequacy, guilt, and fear. I love that You will continue to allow me to be challenged in these areas because I know I will continue to develop integrity. Lord, I love the life you have given me.

RESTLESSNESS

Those times that I spoke of in my journal were times of complete restfulness. I'm sure that in the midst of several of those entries there existed a pile of things I could have been doing: dishes, laundry, exercising. But I felt restful in the knowledge of contentment that *this* was my life. And it was okay with me.

But *restfulness* can turn into *restlessness* in a heartbeat. It's spiritual ADD again, the misfiring of too much ill-directed action.

Like discontentment, restlessness is the empty activity in which we all sometimes take part with no clear purpose. It's an uneasiness and agitation—as if a giant mosquito were buzzing around us, making it impossible to concentrate on being still.

Restlessness in my own life showed during the first ten years of my marriage as I considered a variety of careers as a way to define myself. I enjoyed having my nursing degree, but I wanted more. I wanted head knowledge to give me credibility, to give me a name, to give me a label by which people could *know* what I was. I didn't go back to college after graduating from nursing school, but the different areas I considered pursuing were: nutrition, childbirth education, midwifery, counseling, horse training, horse breeding, teaching, and finally writing (where I have been content for five years!).

This restlessness and uncertainty of "what I should do with my life" could have been avoided if I had seriously consulted the Lord and taken a look at my gifted areas. Though I know I could have "succeeded" in any one of those areas, I wonder if I would have found the restfulness I unconsciously desired. I wanted, no, needed, to find my niche. I believed and claimed Jeremiah 29:11: " 'For I know the plans I have for you,' declares the Lord, 'plans to prosper you and not to harm you, plans to give you a hope and a future.' " This "hope and future" were not going to be born of my own restless desire—they had to come from finding *God's* plan. Even before I actively sought to live in a spirit of stillness, my subconscious knew that was what I felt driven toward.

Restlessly sailing through life without the benefit of God's course sinks a still spirit. Restlessness rocks the boat of stillness, slopping wet, cold waves over you. And the more the boat tips and rocks with your frantic attempts to bail, the more water rushes over the sides. It's hard to restabilize the rocking boat and let tranquillity return. You know what it's like to sit in a tippy canoe—the more you move around, the more tippy it gets. But if you move quietly to the middle and kneel with each arm outstretched to hold the gunnel, the boat stops rocking. Gradually it regains its equilibrium and finally floats quietly on the water.

So it is with restlessness in our walk with God. We're too interested in staying busy, or pursuing head knowledge, or ministering in areas where we aren't gifted. We can't make up our minds about "what to do with my life." A restless walk outside of God's stillness shows us with toes directed indecisively on five different paths.

Eve, too, was restless. First, she was discontent with what she saw as limited access to knowledge. Then after she ate the fruit, she and Adam were banished to fight and scratch for food from the ground itself: " 'Cursed is the ground because of you; through painful toil you will eat of it. . . . By the sweat of your brow you will eat your food' " (Genesis 3:17, 19). Talk about restlessness! Frantic, they had to learn to work the ground and plant their food—no gardening stores nearby or convenient seed packets to order.

That restlessness is still with us today—one of the consequences of original sin. We will always have to grovel for food (whether it's growing our own or going to the grocery store), work to make a living, endure labor to bear children, and struggle to make relationships work. Our lives are difficult!

If we can release that restlessness to the Lord, we will find restfulness. It's a choice. It's letting go and letting God. It's inviting God to steady our restless nature by allowing His plans to come to fruition.

OUR PLANS VS. GOD'S PLANS

During my various flirtings with schemes for my life, I memorized Proverbs 16:1–3. This helped me remember that God's plan was an entire atlas for my life, whereas my plan was merely a ragged map of a one-mile dirt road. "To man belong the plans of the heart, but from the Lord comes the reply of the tongue. All a man's ways seem innocent to him, but motives are weighed by the Lord. Commit to the Lord whatever you do, and your plans will succeed."

Now, a person could take this verse and "commit" an act to the Lord, assuming it will succeed. But I doubt that's what it means— if this were so, we could claim anything, even murder, saying it is okay with God because we've "committed" it to Him. There's danger here. To one who is truly committed to *God* first and has a serious desire to follow God's plan for her life, her motives will be pure, righteous, and God-honoring. A Christian in communion with God would not seek to commit something to the Lord that is outside of God's will.

God's "reply of the tongue" is His answer to the plans of our hearts. He *knows* our hearts—we can't lie to Him, trick Him, or fool Him. So we can go about our schemes and motives and plans, but ultimately they will only come about by the assenting voice of God.

AFFIRM AND CONFIRM

But how exactly do we find God's specific will, His direct path for us? Proverbs 3:5–6 offers guidance: "Trust in the Lord with all your heart and lean not on your own understanding; in all your ways acknowledge him, and he will make your paths straight."

Trust. Oh, but it's hard. Trust that God knows what is best for our children when one of them is struggling with a serious illness. Trust that God will be faithful when our spouse has lost his job. Trust that money will be available for taxes due next week when the savings account is empty today.

There have been times when I've trusted in my mind. Over and over I'll say the words, "I trust You, Lord; I trust You, Lord," only to feel as though my heart isn't hearing the words. Even though I know in my mind that trusting God is the only way my heart has to play catch-up with that knowledge. And that's what the second part of verse 5 means: "Lean not on your own understanding." Why? Because my own understanding will crumble if I lean too hard. My own understanding isn't strong enough to hold me up. My own understanding is built of broken sticks; God's is built of concrete. My own knowledge is too finite to understand how God will act. All I can do is remove my leaning shoulder from my own flimsy, precarious wall and step over to God's trustworthy, solid wall. Phew! This will hold me up!

Before our pastor came to our church, he was the senior pastor of a small but growing congregation. In the midst of ministering with this successful church, he felt God calling him to the military.

Are you kidding? he thought. Married with three children, he questioned why God would ask him to enter the military as a chaplain—traditionally a young single man's role. The answer was simply that God wanted him there. Our pastor did not understand. To him, it made no sense; no human knowledge he possessed could answer the "Why me?" and the "Why now?" He had to completely trust God, not his own understanding. He obeyed and served in the military for seven years, touching thousands of lives all over the world, helping to usher many souls safely into the Lord's hands. He tells of many testimonies of young men coming to the Lord, sometimes just hours before their deaths. He has said it was simultaneously the most challenging and rewarding experience of his life and that of his family. But what if he had not trusted God? What if he had leaned on his own understanding? Many people may well not have heard the gospel. And that would have been tragic.

How can any of us rest in confidence about God's will being done when it doesn't make sense to us as humans? God is omnipotent. What matters is that it makes sense to Him. He sees the whole picture; I see a spot of color. God sees the entire world, each corner, each mountaintop, each ocean depth—all at the same time. All I can see is to the end of my driveway. How, in this limited view of mine, could I trust my own sight more than God's all-encompassing vision? I can't, and furthermore, I don't want to. It makes me feel secure to know that He's indeed holding, guarding, and overseeing the whole world—in His hands. And He has a plan for me and for every person. Wow!

SEEKING GOD'S WILL

I can recall many times when I've had to discern the will of God. From things of great consequence to those of less importance. I remember one such decision was particularly difficult because I was caught up emotionally in the choices I was facing.

When I was hired as a registered nurse to spearhead and act as executive director of a Christian pregnancy care center, I felt called, convicted, and challenged to the job. To me, it seemed to be the ideal position for my life, my skills, and my family. The work was part-time, I had the medical and administrative skills to do it, and I was able to find Christian child care for thirteen-month-old Geneva and later for Jordan when he was born.

I *loved* the job. I developed a vision for the center. I counseled pregnant young women, I trained other counselors, and I built up resources in the community. It was a job of extremes: heartrending stories of broken relationships, dysfunctional families, and crisis pregnancies, as well as the joy of Christ's forgiveness, restored relationships, and the births of healthy babies. But after three years of the emotional demands of the job, I found myself frequently exhausted at home. I prayed for more strength, knowing the Lord could supernaturally boost my energy level. But in my heart, I knew I should be praying for God's direction for my place in the ministry. It was a difficult process. I wanted to stay.

I've had an agreement with the Lord for a number of years. When I ask about a decision, I always pray for the Lord to "affirm and confirm, or deny with closed doors." Being a highly tactile and visual person, I need specifics. God knows that, because He made me this way. He frequently communicates to me through dreams, nature, or literature. I don't feel wrong about asking for specific signs from Him—He has always readily answered me in this regard. So I prayed for the Lord to "affirm and confirm" what I felt He whispered in my heart: *Time to leave.*

First I talked with Peter. Yes, he too saw that I seemed stretched to my limit. Particularly as his business travel away from home was on the rise, he felt I should be more available for the children. Okay, so it had been confirmed by my husband that it was likely the time for me to leave my job.

I hedged, "But what about my income; what about the satisfaction the job gives me? What about the plans I have for the center?

These women *need* me." (A pretty clear correction from the Lord reminded me that, no, they didn't need me, they needed *Him*.)

Then I prayed for specific affirmation from three people so I would be *sure* about leaving. Two affirmations came quickly—from a family member and a close friend. The third surprised me. My collective "bosses" were a board of directors. I had lunch with two of them one day. As I talked about looking for direction about the possibility of leaving the ministry, one of them smiled. She nodded and said, "I've known this was coming. We knew you would leave someday, and though you'll be hard to replace, I agree with your decision to go. Your family needs you more than we do. I want to *affirm* you in that." Perhaps other people use the word "affirm" a lot in casual conversation—but in southern New Hampshire we don't. The use of that specific word cut loose any last grip I had on my job. Now I *knew* the Lord was calling me to back out of the pregnancy center.

I didn't fully understand why I had to leave. God could have given me more strength, and Peter and I could have worked out the issue of his being gone more. But it was clear that it was time for me to leave. If I had leaned on my own understanding, I may well have stayed and compromised my family's well-being—or the functioning of the center itself. Now, in hindsight, I see that if I had leaned on my own vision for the center, it wouldn't have gone in the direction the Lord wanted it to: a center with two offices—one located right next to a college, coordinating a chastity program, operating a clothing exchange for children and pregnant women, and running a post-abortion Bible study. Thank goodness I left. My vision had been much too small! What I saw with my own knowledge and understanding wasn't enough. I didn't have the whole picture.

WE CAN'T IMPRESS GOD

Have you ever found yourself whispering, "See, God, I'll show you what I can do; I'll dazzle You with my works." How vain!! As if we could really teach God something or impress Him.

God is unimpressed with our pursuit of head knowledge. He is the mighty granter of all knowledge—at His discretion and timing. I think it saddens Him when we spend too much time searching for answers that aren't ours to discover. Are we hoping to add to what God already knows? Job puts it succinctly in chapter 21:22: "Can anyone teach knowledge to God, since he judges even the highest?" And in 22:2: "Can a man be of benefit to God? Can even a wise man benefit him?" We can do *nothing* to add to God's knowledge.

We can't change what God knows; we can't alter what God does. Our suggestions for how we'd like Him to do things are vain and ineffective. We can't manipulate God. Our relationship with the Lord is not a tit-for-tat alliance. We can't interfere (nor should we try) with God's divine plan. We can't force His hand, pretending we're playing a giant game of poker. Deuteronomy 10:17 speaks to this: "For the Lord your God is God of gods and Lord of lords, the great God, mighty and awesome, who shows no partiality and accepts no bribes."

It's so tempting to think we can help God along by using our little schemes. Remember Rebekah, mother of Esau and Jacob? She was devoted to her sons and fiercely protective. She had *plans* for her boys. But she had one significant flaw—she loved Jacob more than Esau. Perhaps she viewed him as the underdog because he was the second-born of the twins. Perhaps he wasn't as hearty as Esau, preferring the quiet of home base. But he, along with his mother, was crafty. On the other hand, Esau seemed to care little about his firstborn birthright—when they were younger he tossed it to Jacob in a fit of hunger pangs.

The Lord had spoken to Rebekah when she was pregnant with the twins. He had told her (Genesis 25:23) that the two brothers would be separated. One would be stronger than the other and the younger would rule over the older. The problem was that as the boys' father came close to death, she took it upon herself to implement God's words. For some reason, she thought it was her job to lie, scheme, manipulate, and steal in order for God's prophecy to come true for her boys.

As Isaac aged and became blind, Rebekah felt more and more convinced that Jacob should have the firstborn blessing of his father. She plotted to steal Esau's birthright—even though Jacob resisted. And, indeed, her plan worked: Isaac was tricked into giving Jacob his blessing. The blessing of superior strength, success, and riches. Naturally, Esau was murderously furious when he found out, and Jacob was forced to hide from him.

You have to wonder: Is that the way God would have planned it? I believe God knows what choices we will make for our lives from the moment we are conceived, that He knew this was how Rebekah would weasel the blessing for Jacob. But I wonder what would have been God's plan for Jacob to become ruler over Esau? What would have been His "perfect" way to bring it to pass?

With Rebekah's manipulation came strife, family breakdown, anger, and resentment. In other words, her orchestration only caused problems. So, too, will we find ourselves in a boiling quandary of more problems when we try to "help" God along. Perhaps you've done it in the small things—or maybe in the large things. I know I've tried it, and it never works!

Once again, it comes back to not falling victim to our own finite understanding or knowledge of a situation. We must trust God in His infinite knowledge and vision. I can't even begin to guess what His perfect plan is—my knowledge and vision are too restricted. If I focused on trying to figure out God, searching for definitions of His infiniteness, I couldn't be content. It's not mine to try to figure out. We have each been given the knowledge we need to live the life God has given us. Again, yes, it is good to pursue higher education when God has equipped you and called you to do that. With the degree you earn, you will have responsibilities and opportunities to minister. But I am content knowing God has given me as much knowledge and understanding as I need to impact the lives He intends for me to touch—today and tomorrow. How about you?

Stillness in Action

Write down in which areas of your life you feel discontent: your marriage, your work, your home, other relationships. Try to determine what the root of your dissatisfactions is and write that down, too. Don't hold back. Pour it all out on paper. Then confess any sin that may be involved. Follow this by praying, "I am content knowing that You know what is best for me, Lord." Repeat this prayer every time you start to feel discontentment threatening your inner stillness.

MEMORY VERSE

"But the plans of the Lord stand firm forever, the purposes of his heart through all generations."

PSALM 33:11

Heart Knowledge

"Surely you desire truth in the inner parts;
you teach me wisdom in the inmost place."

P S A L M   5 1 : 6

As I mentioned earlier, one of the gifts the Lord has entrusted
to me is discernment. I see things in people. I not only know when
they are hurting inside, I feel their pain and can frequently discern
the root from which their pain stems. I've recognized family alco-
holism as the seed of bitterness displayed in others. I've seen guilt
as the innermost core of those who like to point their finger in blame
of others. In my previous work at the Christian life-affirming pregnancy center, I could almost invariably pick out the women who had
abortion histories, even as they walked through the counseling center's door. I could see the hurts, the pain, and the spiritual history
of some as though they were carrying a sign around their neck for
all to read.

On a crisp fall day I'd stopped at the small market near our home for a few items. As I was leaving, a young woman started up the sloped entryway. Her short, bright-orange hair seemed a little out-of-place for our small, conservative town. She kept her eyes down, shuffled up the ramp, squeezed her heavyset frame past me, and mumbled "thanks" as I held the door for her. Before I had even stepped off the ramp, two thoughts came to me: I was the only person that day who had shown her kindness—by holding the door for her—and she felt extremely alone because people had been teasing her. I sat in my car and said a silent prayer for her. As I turned the ignition key, I saw the same young lady come out of the store. She walked to the car next to mine. As she reached for her car door, I noticed for the first time that the driver's side was covered with smashed bits of rotting apples. When she opened her door, a small piece slid down onto her hand. I saw her shoulders rise, perhaps in anger or irritation. Then she shook it off, wiped her hand across her jeans, and got into her car. Then she saw me watching her. She quickly glanced away, a touch of pink on her cheeks. I gave her a little smile, put my car in drive, and drove away.

I prayed more fervently for her, that God would reveal himself to her in the midst of her loneliness. I realized I'd not only witnessed a fragment of the embarrassment and humiliation this girl was feeling, but I'd seen it clinging to her before I even noticed the defamation to her car. What I did with the glimpse I had been given into her heart is where God's wisdom comes in. I could have driven away thinking, *Hmmm, that's too bad.* But I've learned that with the gift of discernment, or any gift, comes responsibility. The wisdom that I have through discernment sometimes leads me to simply say a silent prayer, as I did for the outcast young woman. Other times it might nudge me to say something. There have been times when I've noticed something going on in an acquaintance's life and I'll send her an encouraging note. How do I know how to respond in each situation? By praying for God's wisdom to show me how to use the heart knowledge He has granted me. His wisdom is the avenue by which to minister to others; I'm just a vessel.

HOW HEART KNOWLEDGE IS DIFFERENT FROM HEAD KNOWLEDGE

In the last chapter, we talked about head knowledge being limited by our humanity. We aren't meant to understand in our heads how God works. But in our hearts God can give us pure, sometimes sudden knowledge about a situation or circumstance. It's a feeling of *I know that I know that I know.*

We also have the responsibility to look for opportunities to use this "knowing." Emilie Griffin discusses studying God's Word for knowledge, and says, "Study, then, implies not only application but also attentiveness; the mind must be prepared to read between the lines of existence, grasping the unstated meaning of every text."[1] Indeed, every text and circumstance. It was as if I saw on the young woman leaving the convenience store a transparent shield that revealed the pain etched on her heart.

Heart knowledge is the internal assurance and use of God's wisdom. As we talk about heart knowledge, you'll feel the stillness of "Be still, and know that I am God" taking root in your heart. The stillness starts in the recesses of your heart. As you see the capability God has given your heart to know and understand, you will be able to remain still in Him.

A WOMAN'S "KNOWING"

I have a deep and stubborn belief in a woman's innate capabilities. I have been witness over and over to the impact of a woman's finely tuned discernment. Women are capable of noticing nuances, spoken and unspoken, that are foreign to and elude men. I'm not male bashing here. I'm explaining what I see as an extra sensitivity that God gave to women. Some might call this a woman's sixth sense. I call it female radar.

A tuned-in woman's radar picks up faint blips in the periphery. That's why women are frequently finding careers in the "helps" fields—medicine, counseling, teaching, etc. Women are in tune with low-flying, high-flying, and masked emotions. They can decipher and read it all correctly. This is why it is also my conviction that a woman's innate knowing should be a part of every church leadership team. A woman with clear discernment sees the peripheral and subtle changes in the church body. She offers balance to a man's more focused approach.

Men operate from a rational side. Men look at facts. Women look at facts *and* the reason the facts came to be *and* the result of the facts on people. They have a deeper understanding of the reason for and the effect of situations. This is how God made women.

When Jordan was six years old, Peter bought tickets for the two of them to attend a hockey game in downtown Boston. I felt dubious. My mother's instinct (or woman's knowing) was that a hockey game might not be the best place for a tender child of six. What started as my initial cautionary "be careful" to Peter about Jordan's impressionability ended in a hurtful argument about having wisdom and discernment in raising our children. I accused Peter of being blind and naïve about the influences to which Jordan would be exposed. Peter accused me of being overprotective, having an overactive imagination, and trying to rob him of father/son time with Jordan.

We both knew we wanted the same things for Jordan—for him to grow into a godly man with personal, faith-based convictions, with loving memories of his family, and with compassion for others. The problem was that Peter and I weren't connected on how to help Jordan reach those end results.

During our heated argument, I reminded Peter in a not-so-gentle manner that God had given *me* discernment about our kids. I embellished on the times I'd been *right* about deciphering subtleties in our children's lives.

Peter remained unconvinced, likely because of the way I said it. They went to the game, had a great time, and Jordan returned with wide eyes and a whole new vocabulary.

See, I told you so! No, seriously. I had been right. My approach and word choices were very wrong, but I had known that a hockey game wasn't the best environment for a susceptible young child from the hills of New Hampshire.

Peter had seen the opportunity as a fun sporting event to enjoy with his son—and that is all. I saw the potential ramifications of the whole experience. He was focused on the game itself; I was focused on the effect of the environment on our son. I had to gently remind Jordan that taking God's name in vain was disrespectful, that the use of his middle finger alone was inappropriate, and that fistfighting wasn't an answer to an argument with his sister.

Call it maternal instinct, a woman's knowing, or wisdom. The point is that as women and mothers, we have an extra sense about many things—not just our children.

The verse cited at the beginning of this chapter speaks of "truth in the inner parts, the inmost place." In the physical body, this is your heart—that's why God designed it to be protected by your rib cage. Likewise, your spiritual heart is the core of your personal convictions and faith. A woman's attentive knowing is born from this core.

Maybe you feel that God overlooked the investment of discernment in you. I guarantee you that's not true. I am convinced that a measure of discernment is part of every woman's makeup. But it may take some work on your part to be sure discernment and wisdom have a place to grow in your heart.

When spiritual ADD is present in your life, it keeps knocking down the growth that God starts in your heart. Remember the image of spiritual ADD with outstretched arms banging into everything in your life? But when you have the beginning roots of stillness, as I hope you do now from reading this book, there's more room for

God to grow wisdom and discernment in your heart and life. Spiritual ADD and discernment are incompatible with each other. As you develop a closer walk with the Lord and learn to be still in Him, you'll find that your discernment increases because you're less distractible.

GUILTY HEARTS

It sounds easy, doesn't it—to invite stillness into our hearts and ask it to reside there in peace? The problem is that there are sometimes obstacles in our lives that block the entrance of stillness. Let me tell you a story.

I'm a person who feels guilty a lot. I will apologize for the weather if given a chance. I say I'm sorry for things that have nothing to do with me.

My guilt is born of a deep desire for truth gone awry. It all goes back to an event in my childhood when I let my naturally guilty conscious get a little out of hand. I got caught shoplifting when I was a young teen—an ice cream bar. I left the wrapper in the trash outside the back door of the little store; I'd never make a good robber. Though restitution meant paying for the bar, apologizing to the storekeeper, and confessing to my parents, it was enough to make me never want to steal again. Consequently, to this day when I'm in a store, I find myself unconsciously holding my purchases out in front of me. I don't put my hands in my pockets. And I feel guilty if a salesperson looks at me. It's as if I must constantly defend myself and my honesty in everyone's presence. My featherlight brush with stealing imprinted a deep sense of shame on my heart. It has taken me years to recognize it and deal with it.

Unfortunately, there have been other sins in my life that are also worthy of my shame and guilt. Mistreatment of others, judging people according to how they look, gossip, courting flirtatious behavior, lying about situations. You, too, know your vulnerable areas. Those thoughts that you mask from others. Perhaps there is dishonesty, lust, cursing, hitting, gluttony. I don't need to go on. I don't want to point a finger at you—you likely do enough self-finger-pointing. You don't need me to show you the areas of guilt in your life.

I carried a heavy guilt with me for three years concerning a time when I had lied about and manipulated a situation. I kept quietly justifying it over and over to myself. But the more I did this, the more guilty I felt. I feared being "found out." I asked the Lord to remove my guilt and fear. Though I knew in my mind that He had indeed forgiven and forgotten my error, I knew I needed to do more to remove my self-incrimination. I felt that if I were to come to terms with what I had done, I needed to confess it out loud to a friend.

I sat on the edge of the bed of a very dear and very safe friend. I had told her about my need to talk—that I needed to share something with someone, so she was prepared. I fell backward across the bed, my arms outstretched as if I was about to make an angel mark on her quilt. Then I poured out my heart. I confessed what I felt my wrong had been. I sobbed, and she held my hand. Then she gently stroked my hair and reminded me of the good that had come from the situation, that despite my sin and guilt, "God works for the good of those who love him" (Romans 8:28). She said that even though I had sinned, God made something good of my mistake because I remained "in Christ Jesus" past, present, and future. I blinked and said, "Oh, yeah."

Her wise words comforted me and rerouted my thought pattern. I had been unable to look past my error to see anything positive. I had found myself so deep in the mud of guilt that I hadn't seen the life-saving vine of Christ's forgiveness over my head.

A few days later I came across Colossians 1:22: "But now he has reconciled you by Christ's physical body through death to present you holy in his sight, *without blemish and free from accusation*" (italics mine). What a profound relief and conclusion to my confession.

With this verse I could turn the page on that particular guilt. Case closed.

Guilt can be a weighty stone around your neck that you have allowed to remain even after you've asked for Christ's forgiveness. Unresolved guilt leads to blame. Blaming others, blaming yourself, blaming God. Blame is a form of self-bondage. With the weight of the guilt-bondage stone dragging at your every move, you become exhausted. It becomes such an effort to move through your life— making decisions, acting responsibly, working in ministry. You may find yourself struggling against the confining hold of bondage, adding to your overall spiritual exhaustion.

When you've asked for forgiveness, Christ himself cuts the cords of bondage. He sets you free. Guess what? Now you don't need to struggle and fight against the ropes. Your spiritual energy can return. You may feel weak from the struggle, but now you can rest quietly next to your Savior. If you still tremble with the aftershocks of bondage, commit Colossians 1:22–23 to memory. Verse 23 is so comforting: ". . . if you continue in your faith, established and firm, not moved from the hope held out in the gospel." How reassuring to know that the Lord is not pointing an accusing finger at us. Because of Christ's forgiveness and the freedom that comes with forgiveness, we are "not moved" (we can be still!) as the Lord holds out the lifeline of His Word.

In this we can rest in confidence. Stillness of spirit is the by-product of releasing guilt.

FEARFUL HEARTS

I've already talked a bit about fear and losing control to the Lord. I'd like to share another story with you about a deep-seated fear I struggled with for many years.

I had been unnaturally afraid of germs. I panicked over the thought of getting sick. I had an incapacitating anxiety of breathing the same air as strangers. All I could envision were air particles

bearing germs ready for me to inhale. I'm not talking about a simple
dislike of the inconvenience of an illness, I'm talking about a fear so
devastating I cringed to hug or kiss my own kids for fear of catching
an illness they might have been harboring.

I know somehow that this didn't jibe with my nursing career,
but my illness paranoia was partly what had caused me to leave tra-
ditional nursing in pursuit of the administrative job at the pregnancy center. Because of my fear, I found myself holding my breath
in crowds, leaving me feeling lightheaded, weak, and nauseated. I
knew I was treading an emotionally unhealthy path, and I wanted
to be free from my ever-increasing panic.

I prayed for healing and I memorized Scripture. As I was reading
through Acts, I came across the account of Peter's arrest and miraculous escape from prison (Acts 12:1–19). It seemed to me that
Peter would have been terrified when the angel came and "struck
[him] on the side and woke him up." But Peter didn't hesitate to
follow the angel's directions, and he stood up, got dressed, and followed.

I felt a flicker of recognition in these verses. I, too, was chained
in my prison of fear, and God had come to me, telling me to "get
up." "But how do I 'get up,' Lord?" I asked. My prison of fear had
become a familiar place. Despite the cold and discomfort of its confines, I knew it all too well. I knew the dark, grimy walls and the
rank smell. In its own way my jail felt "safe." But the Lord impressed
upon me again, "Get up."

I knew the Lord could heal with a simple divine whisper, but I
also knew that frequently the Lord allows me to grow out of my
issues. He placed growth opportunities in my life to enable me to
take steps toward healing. I found that these were the avenues by
which He wanted me to "get up." I started meeting with a small
group of women as an accountability group. My friends served to
help me keep my eyes focused on Christ as I muddled my way
toward healing. I also worked part-time for a caterer, serving people

at weddings and family get-togethers. For me, this was a giant step toward freedom—to be able to handle silverware that had been in someone else's mouth seemed a giant obstacle overcome.

During this nearly two-year struggle to get out of my self-prison, I came to realize that my God-given nature will always be reserved in crowds and groups; it was okay to feel inhibited, as long as I didn't let my reservation turn into a panic that ruled my life. The final breakthrough from my jail of fear came when I accepted the fact that the short time I may actually have an illness was insignificant compared to the long-term imprisonment of fear. I would rather have freedom from my prison and take the chance of getting sick than be permanently bound by panic.

The verses in Acts 12 tell about Peter's report to his friends who had been praying for his release from prison. Rhoda, the young woman who answered Peter's knock, was so overjoyed, and the astonished people were making so much noise about Peter's liberation, that he told them to be quiet. The joy of freedom was contagious. I agree. That joy is something worth catching!

What are some of the deep-rooted fears in your life? With the heart knowledge God is growing in you, your fears have no room to continue. This heart knowledge will help you to discern what roots of fear need to be weeded from your heart. The fears must be acknowledged, confessed, and tossed aside. As I learned from Peter's prison release, the Lord wants you, too, to "get up" so you can be free to fear no more.

Psalm 27:1 helps put fear in its proper perspective: "The Lord is my light and salvation—whom shall I fear? The Lord is the stronghold of my life—of whom shall I be afraid?" Indeed, God himself is in charge; there can be no circumstance or fear in your life too big for Him to heal.

HEART KNOWLEDGE OPENS YOUR EYES

Our eternal salvation rests on Christ's death and resurrection. The four accounts in the Gospels relay four different versions of

Christ's reappearance after His death. Each one speaks of doubt about Jesus' return to life.

Initially the disciples didn't recognize Jesus when He rose from the dead. Even though He had told them He would be back, they couldn't believe their eyes when He did indeed appear. Up until Jesus' death they had tangible, tactile evidence of Him. It was almost easy to follow Him—they could *see* Him. Now, post-crucifixion, they would have to rely on the knowledge they had in their hearts of Christ. Their heart knowledge meant that their eyes were now opened to the needs of others without Christ being physically present to direct them. In Mark 16:15, Christ commissions them to "Go into all the world and preach the good news." In this the disciples were given heart knowledge, a God-given discernment and ability to perform miracles in His name.

I am also reminded of Paul's conversion to Christianity (Acts 22:1–21). Paul, previously named Saul, had persecuted the followers of Christ: arresting them, imprisoning them, torturing them. While Saul was en route to Damascus to capture more Christians, Christ himself flashed a blazing light on Saul's sin. Saul was blinded and thrown to the ground by the intensity of the encounter. Even before any words were spoken by the Lord, Saul recognized the brilliance as God himself when he asked, "Who are you, Lord?" After being hand-led by his companions to Damascus, Saul's sight returned by God's healing through the presence and words of Ananias. Ananias confirmed that Saul had been chosen to "know his will and to see the Righteous One and to hear words from his mouth." With these words, Saul suddenly had been granted heart knowledge: the knowledge of the omnipotence of God.

NO PRIDE

Before Paul's conversion, pride motivated him. He acted arrogantly, thinking he had greater intelligence and power than the Christians. After the Lord deftly put Saul in his place and changed his name to Paul, pride melted away. Now he was an ambassador of the Almighty, and nothing others could do, say, or threaten, would change the humility by which Paul was now motivated.

Pride is not compatible with God-given heart knowledge, because the more we know about God, who He is, and how He functions, the more humbled we become. The fact that *God* can use *us*—in our finite limitations—to glorify Him should only send us to our knees in God-adoring humility. Psalm 131:1 confirms this, saying, "My heart is not proud, O Lord, my eyes are not haughty; I do not concern myself with great matters or things too wonderful for me."

Inner pride blocks God's self-revealing knowledge. In what areas of your life do you hold God at arm's length? Perhaps you think you know what's best in a situation, or you are too proud to acknowledge that you don't know the answer to something or how to deal with a circumstance.

I confess to pride in my life. I can think of a painful time in the not-too-distant past when I was dealing with an issue with my son, Jordan. I tried to go it alone, trying to be a Lone Ranger in my hurt and confusion. Growing up as a staunch New Englander, I learned you never ask for help. Call it Yankee pride or stubbornness—in this particular situation I found it overwhelmingly difficult to reach out for help. I kept a stiff upper lip, while my heart felt as if it were shrinking and receding from God.

Until a hymn at church broke my wall of pride. The words in the third verse of "He Leadeth Me" end with "through Jordan He leadeth me." Fist clenched to my mouth, I ran from the sanctuary to the ladies' room. God was definitely leading me somewhere through the situation with my son, Jordan. As my hurt and tears tumbled down at my feet, a woman I barely knew came in to ask if I was okay. "No," I croaked. She rubbed the back of my shoulder as I sobbed and sobbed. Finally I poured out the story to her. The whole time I talked, the word "pride" kept coming to my mind. In one last choking gulp I said, "And it's been pride that has stopped me from asking for help, from admitting I needed help." She nodded knowingly. Then she asked if she could pray for me. "Yes, please," I said simply. In my acceptance of her prayer, I felt the rest of my pride melt away. It's not that she said anything profound or revealing, it was simply the gentleness by which her prayer was ministered. I felt God's sure peace return with the conviction that yes, indeed, even through this painful time, He was still in control. I left church thinking to myself, *Why didn't I ask for help sooner? I could have benefited from this peace weeks ago!*

As I learned, the churning, self-righteous attitude of pride cannot coexist with a still spirit. Psalm 51:17 reads, "The sacrifices of God are a broken spirit; a broken and contrite heart, O God, you will not despise." My heart had needed a good dose of contriteness! Once my eyes were opened to the pride I harbored in my heart, the Lord could teach me something. Then He could, indeed, lead me "through Jordan."

PLAYING SEEK AND FIND

Gaining heart knowledge does require some action on our part. As I found in the situation about Jordan, I needed to reach out and ask for help. Relying on myself made the circumstance more painful. Reaching out diffused my pain. I learned that I must seek out ways in which I can learn heart knowledge. I did myself a disservice by not allowing God to teach me through Jordan at the outset.

Second Chronicles, chapters 14–16, discusses the reign of King Asa in the land of Judah. For thirty-five years Asa governed as a godly man and ruler. He encouraged his people to follow the one and only God, he tore down idols, and he made laws in the Lord's favor. At one point he declared an assembly in Jerusalem to declare a covenant to "seek the Lord." Verse 15 of chapter 15 says, "All Judah rejoiced about the oath because they had sworn it wholeheartedly. They sought God eagerly, and he was found by them. So the Lord gave them rest on every side." If only we, too, could see the intense need for and benefit from seeking the Lord "wholeheartedly," because we see clearly in this verse that the result will be "rest on every side." Yes, indeed, complete restfulness and stillness!

Seeking God to gain a heart of knowledge is a lifelong endeavor. Knowledge is an offshoot of the vine of wisdom that you are growing in your life. Just as wisdom will grow for as long as you nurture it, so, too, will knowledge grow as you tend it. Plucking and removing dead issues in your life, feeding the roots of your faith with personal Bible study, and offering ever bigger containers in which to grow your gifts, your heart knowledge will increase and spread.

Stillness in Action

Try this exercise as an ongoing reminder of God's heart knowledge and wisdom growing in your life. Buy yourself a small plant, or clip a small root off an existing plant and replant it. Place it where you'll see it during your quiet times or while journaling. Name it Wisdom or Knowledge (or any other name you'd like) and tend to its needs. Take a picture of it when you first purchase it, and again in six months, then again in a year. Compare the growth rates, and consider the symbolism in your life! You may feel as though you have black thumbs and will surely kill any living plant entrusted to your hands. I have felt that way, too. Be sure to buy a plant that suits the spot where it will reside, and ask for help from a nursery to ensure its growth. Even if it fades away, don't despair. Buy a new one. Remember, we are all new creatures in Christ!

MEMORY VERSE

"The advantage of knowledge is this: that wisdom preserves the life of its possessor."

ECCLESIASTES 7:12

CHAPTER NINE

God Knowledge

"Oh, the depth of the riches of
the wisdom and knowledge of God!"

ROMANS 11:33

I love chocolate. To me, it is the pinnacle of mouth-watering sensations. It has made me feel better when I've been depressed; it's been my friend when I've been lonely; it's been a partner in times of celebration. I used to be capable of eating an entire quart of Ben and Jerry's New York Super Fudge Chunk ice cream in one sitting.

Then I hit my mid-thirties. It seemed that my body suddenly switched on a panic button and shut down my tolerance for fat-laden foods, lactose, and chocolate. Boy, did I resist this. I persisted in trying to eat chocolate and ice cream only to find myself wretchedly ill afterward. How I resented giving up my comfort foods! But I realized my body just couldn't take it anymore. My gallbladder couldn't process the fat, my intestines couldn't break down the lactose, and my entire body rejected the chocolate. My years of overeating chocolate turned out to be too much of a good thing.

I feel empathy toward how Eve felt when she was told explicitly not to eat the fruit of a particular tree. (Was there such a thing as chocolate on trees in the Garden of Eden?) The fruit would prove to be too much of a good thing. It looked to be a good tree: pleasant to look at and the fruit an attractive color. It even promised to give knowledge and wisdom if ingested—a good thing, right?

Wrong.

After tasting the fruit of the forbidden tree, Adam and Eve suddenly did have knowledge—knowledge of their unsightly humanity. Did it give them what the serpent had promised: "You will be like God, knowing good and evil" (Genesis 3:5)? In a certain respect it did give them more godlike knowledge. God's perfect plan, pre-Fall, would have been for Adam and Eve to remain ignorant of sin and temptation; post-Fall they suddenly had the understanding of good—God's perfect goodness, and of evil—Satan's deceptive lies. So when God banished them, they no longer could have Eden-pure goodness—they were stripped of that privilege.

Through Christ our Redeemer, we once again have access to God the Father. We aren't meant to know, understand, or comprehend God's absolute knowledge. We wouldn't have a need for Him if we did. We're looking at a bit of a two-sided drama, however. On the one side, we can't possibly gain the full knowledge of God, but on the other side, as Christians, we can't live in the absence of the influence of God's knowledge. As Tony Evans so succinctly puts it in *Our God Is Awesome,* "Our brains are too small, our knowledge too limited, ourselves too finite to live life the way it was meant to be lived apart from the knowledge of God."[1]

The human heart and head knowledge that we've looked at in the two preceding chapters give us a clear—albeit distant—view of God's infinite knowledge. The knowledge of God is the end result. As we have seen, this knowledge is for our own edification as well as that of others. God knowledge is knowing God for the sake of knowing God—or the characteristics that make Him God. That is, the very nature of God; His ways, His motives, His holiness, His being. This knowledge cannot be pure—our view will always be somewhat nearsighted because of our ever-present humanity—but pursuing wisdom through head and heart knowledge will give us a divine glimmer of the mind of God.

JESUS IS THE AVENUE TO GOD KNOWLEDGE

One of my favorite questions to ask my close friends who are sisters in Christ is, "So, what has the Lord been doing in your life lately?" What follows is usually a time of sharing deep spiritual intimacies that invariably touch me and minister to me. What I also notice so often is that a few of my friends are at similar places in their walks with the Lord. So it came as no surprise when a dear friend shared with two of us that she felt the Lord drawing her closer to Him. It echoed the very things I was writing about in this book. My friend sighted the account of the Samaritan woman at the well as an example of His desire to draw us closer to himself.

John 4:4–26 relays this remarkable conversation. First, the Samaritan woman is shy about Jesus asking her for a drink—Jews and Samaritans did not publicly speak to each other. Then she gets a little argumentative with Jesus; what was he trying to tell her about "living water"? Then she felt wonder; she wanted this eternal thirst quencher. Next, when Jesus confronted her, she felt remorse about living with a man who was not her husband. But, finally, she felt profound awe and belief—this man called himself the Christ and knew her whole life story!

Jesus drew the Samaritan woman in, engaging her in conversation, enticing her with His words. His knowledge intrigued her. He met her at her point of need. I imagine at first the woman was standing at a bit of a distance, skeptical about His motives. But, as they talked, I can see her taking a few steps forward until she was face-to-face with Him—holding an intelligent, meaningful conversation.

And *she* a known sinner and social outcast!

Aren't we the same way? Maybe a bit standoffish at first—dubious of what His demands of us will be? But all He wants to do—as with the woman at the well—is to draw us in, draw us closer, to commune with Him. The Samaritan woman was deeply touched and immediately equipped to go and tell others. First, she had to spend time in conversation with Him, then His words prepared her to go and tell what she had discovered.

That's pretty immediate God knowledge, wouldn't you say? The order of events is so important: first, we must be drawn in. Next, we must converse and commune with Christ, and then we will be equipped with God's firsthand knowledge.

First Corinthians 1:30 says, "It is because of him that you are in Christ Jesus, who has become for us wisdom from God." And Ephesians 1:17: "I keep asking that the God of our Lord Jesus Christ, the glorious Father, may give you the Spirit of wisdom and revelation, so that you may know him better." Both of these verses tell us God's wisdom and knowledge come through our personal relationship with Christ.

In Philippians 3:10, Paul laments, "I want to know Christ and the power of his resurrection and the fellowship of sharing in his sufferings, becoming like him." Paul felt this was the only important thing in his life—to share in who Christ is and what He did. All of his writings capture the same feeling—a desire to draw closer to Christ and to take on more of His characteristics.

These Christlike characteristics, to which we aspire in our desire to gain God knowledge, are nowhere more efficiently highlighted than in 2 Peter 1:5–8:

> For this very reason, make every effort to add to your faith goodness; and to goodness, knowledge; and to knowledge, self-control; and to self-control, perseverance; and to perseverance, godliness; and to godliness, brotherly kindness; and to brotherly

kindness, love. For if you possess these qualities in increasing measure, they will keep you from being ineffective and unproductive in your knowledge of our Lord Jesus Christ.

In other words, the more we can grow in and claim these qualities in our Christian walk, the more of God's knowledge we will have, because we will be taking on the very nature of Christ himself!

DISTINGUISHING GOOD FROM EVIL

Part of becoming more Christlike is an ability to *see* what is Christlike and what is not. This knowledge is part of God knowledge, knowing what is of God and what is not.

I'd like to believe every person is always 100 percent honest. I would have been a good defense attorney: I like to assume someone is innocent until proven guilty. It's only been in recent years that I've taken on a more suspicious view of the world: sometimes I wonder about people's motives. I hesitate about things that seem too good to be true. Nevertheless, for a number of years I blindly assumed that all people of faith were as 100 percent committed to their relationship with the Lord as I was. I'd always had a particularly naïve perspective about "Christians." Some, of course, I could tell were inauthentic from the second they spoke, but others, I really liked to give the benefit of the doubt, even when I'd had internal red flags flapping in my mind. Instead of questioning their intent, I began to doubt my own discernment, because I had viewed them as more "spiritual" than I felt I was. I'd think, *Surely they must be right and I must be wrong!*

I learned the extremely painful and hard way that some Christians can be the most deceptive—and the scary realization is that they are very good at their deception and manipulation.

I saw a Christian counselor off and on for about five years shortly before I was married and into the first several years of my marriage—most of my issues were esteem- and fear-related. This highly regarded man had various degrees and was a gifted teacher and counselor. A number of my friends, male and female, also counseled with him. As one of the avenues to help me explore my low esteem and fears, he encouraged me to keep a journal about my daily life and walk with the Lord. I gladly complied—I loved to write. He asked if he could read what I'd written, and though I felt a little uncomfortable, I allowed him to page through the entries. In hindsight, I see this as one of the first violations that led to other violations. They were comparatively small things, but when looked at together added up to serious breaches of conduct. Inside my heart I kept feeling, *This doesn't seem right, something seems off here.* But those feelings never really rose to a conscious thought until much later. Every time I felt even a second's hesitation in my spirit, I'd close the shutter on my discernment; not a conscious thought escaped to allow a warning. After all, he was a professional—right?

About three years after I stopped seeing him, one of his counselees accused him of sexual misconduct. Then another came forward, then another, then another—until it became known that there were several women with whom he had committed adultery. A big "Now, I see" on my part! At the same time, however, I felt chagrined. I had indeed felt something amiss when I visited him as a client those years before—but I hadn't had enough confidence in myself and my tender discernment to really acknowledge or act on those feelings.

Did I even form a prayer when I had those flashes of misgivings? No. Did I talk with other women who were seeing him about their counseling times with him? No. Did I talk with my husband about my fleeting feelings of discomfort? No. Did I ask for more discernment to be able to distinguish if what I was feeling was true or false? No. My question to myself now is, knowing that I wasn't nearly as spiritually mature then as I am now (and admitting I still have a very long way to go!), what would it have taken for me to acknowledge and act on the counselor's misconduct? My answer is, *a deep enough knowledge of God himself and a confidence in the ability He has given me to discern good from evil.*

Again, the obvious benefit of drawing closer to Christ and seeing a broader view of God's knowledge is the ability to know what is of God and what isn't. Proverbs 14:6 says, "The mocker seeks wisdom and finds none, but knowledge comes easily to the discerning." Comes "easily"? Yes, but with practice. This ability to distinguish *God* as the source of something as opposed to any other influence comes with *confidence* and stillness of spirit, which we gain from spending time with the Lord. There is a threefold process that helps to grow discernment and then find confidence in it. Once again, the stillness we are ultimately seeking first requires action.

ARMORING

In chapter 5 we looked at Ephesians 6:14–17, which talks about protecting ourselves with the "full armor of God."

Let's read it again: "Stand firm then, with the belt of truth buckled around your waist, with the breastplate of righteousness in place, and with your feet fitted with the readiness that comes from the gospel of peace. In addition to all this, take up the shield of faith, with which you can extinguish all the flaming arrows of the evil one. Take the helmet of salvation and the sword of the Spirit, which is the word of God."

My mom taught me to recite these verses each morning as a prayer to start my day. It's a form of spiritual protection and a reminder to carry the shield of Christ throughout the day. So we've put the armor on, but what exactly are we so concerned about in the first place that we need armor? Good point. We need to know what we're armoring ourselves against before the process can be useful. Blithely clothing ourselves with these protective shields will only be as effective as we are educated about the forms of attack that will be waged against us.

These verses from Ephesians tell us we are arming ourselves

against "the flaming arrows of the evil one." Look at this with me literally for a moment. When I think of flaming arrows, I see a pitch-black night enveloping a fortress. I see guards atop a wall, on the lookout and listening for intruders. Then I hear the war cries of invaders and see streams of flames shooting through the sky to the wood-framed, highly combustible structure. The attackers simultaneously shoot to kill the guards on the wall and fire into the hinged front gates. Fiery arrows torch the structure, killing, scarring, damaging, destroying all inside.

That's exactly the picture we need to have in our mind's eye when we consider how swiftly and completely an attack can be commandeered by Satan. He is usually subtle—just a flicker of fear or doubt about a circumstance in our lives. Other times he might be more persuasive, and perhaps we rationalize our actions with "No one will know if I cheat a little, or disobey the law, or think about another man," allowing the torch of temptation a direct route through the gate of our heart to the very soul of our inner being. Regardless of how or when he attacks, it's guaranteed that he is always planning an attack. Hence the need for full protection with the full armor of God all the time! It's often said that if you're feeling under attack by Satan—you must be doing something right in your Christian walk.

DISTINGUISHING

For the protection of the armor of God to work, you need to identify your weakest areas. The saying goes: A chain is only as strong as its weakest link. So with you, any attack will be directed at your weakest area. I know too well what my weakest areas are: the armpit of fear, the exposed jugular of self-doubt, and the bared flank of self-control. What are yours?

Distinguishing and discernment go hand in hand. Discernment clues you in to something out of place—a spiritual red flag of caution. Distinguishing takes this a step further—it helps you to determine exactly what is or isn't of God. Proverbs 28:11 says, "A rich man may be wise in his own eyes, but a poor man who has discernment sees through him." Discernment and the ability to distinguish good from evil are only dependent on a willingness to use these gifts given by God in a measure to all of us. As with wisdom, they are not necessarily an old man's inheritance or a rich man's privilege. But they do require a willingness and desire to be growing spiritually mature. Hebrews 5:14 says, "But solid food is for the mature, who by constant use have trained themselves to distinguish good from evil."

In Philippians 1:9–10, Paul reminds us to pray for increasing measures of discernment and distinguishing skills so that we personally can turn from sin: "And this is my prayer: that your love may abound more and more in knowledge and depth of insight, so that you may be able to discern what is best and may be pure and blameless until the day of Christ." This brings us back to knowing your weakest points—your areas of vulnerability, which Satan also knows all too well. If you take these words of Paul to heart, you can apply your growing distinguishing abilities to your own life. We can and should ask for a glaring light to illuminate our weakest areas. How else can we know what to arm ourselves against?

HANDLING

Second Timothy 2:15 reminds us, "Do your best to present yourself to God as one approved, a workman who does not need to be ashamed and who correctly handles the word of truth." As we identify and distinguish those areas we need to be guarded about, we become more "approved" in God's eyes: dying to self and living in Christ. In this place, we have become capable of "handling the word of truth." We are mature enough, trusting enough, and spiritually wise enough to handle God knowledge.

Moses is a great example of handling God knowledge. Remember how Moses had a serious identity crisis when God asked him to

lead the Israelites out of Egypt? Talk about a lack of confidence—
basically he kept saying, "Who, ME?!" God had to reveal himself in
a miraculous way for skeptical Moses to believe and act according
to the Lord's command to him. Exodus 4:2–4 relays the first part of
the signs that God gave Moses as proof of His awesome power:

> Then the Lord said to him, "What is that in your hand?" "A
> staff," he replied. The Lord said, "Throw it on the ground."
> Moses threw it on the ground and it became a snake, and he
> ran from it. Then the Lord said to him, "Reach out your hand
> and take it by the tail." So Moses reached out and took hold of
> the snake and it turned back into a staff in his hand.

It's important to note that Moses' staff is indeed the "staff of
God" (as noted later in verse 20). Because there was no written Word
of God then as there is today, that staff had God's truth as part of
its makeup. Just as our Bibles today are the undeniable Word of the
Lord, so too was Moses' staff the undeniable avenue of the Word of
the Lord to be used as proof for the Israelites.

When Moses threw the staff on the ground and it turned into a
snake, he did the only thing most rational humans would do—run!
But God told him to pick it up by the *tail*—a bold invitation to be
bitten. I can imagine Moses stopping in his retreating tracks, turning
around to face the snake, his heart racing, reaching out—perhaps
holding his breath, afraid he'll be bitten, then snatching the snake's
tail. What relief when it instantly turned back into the staff—God's
steady rod of correction.

Talk about "handling the truth"! What can we learn from Moses
grabbing hold of the snake's tail (staff)? If you take hold of God's
Word with full force, knowing there will be complete assurance of
protection, tempered with respect for the power of the truth, then
it will become your guide, strength, and avenue to God's knowledge.

The threefold process of armoring, distinguishing, and finally
handling brings us to a point where we are prepared to be obedient

to God's leading. Because now we have confidence in hearing God's directives, much as Moses learned. In other words, we are simultaneously competent and vulnerable. We are equipped to fight for our faith, but tender to the Lord's touch. We have the personal conviction that we can handle whatever the Lord brings our way. Now we can expectantly wait for Him to reveal himself. And we know that this sometimes requires stillness!

DIVINE REVELATIONS

Habakkuk the prophet is an example of prepared waiting for God's revelation—the revelation of God's plan, purpose, and divine knowledge.

Habakkuk was concerned about what he saw happening in Judah—injustice and violence. He petitioned the Lord about this, and thus begins the book that documents their "conversation."

Habakkuk doesn't understand why the Lord is answering him the way He does; He will bring justice through an even more violent people—the Babylonians. Yet in 2:1 the prophet says, "I will stand watch and station myself on the ramparts; I will look to see what he will say to me, and what answer I am to give to this complaint." Then in verse 3 the Lord answers Habakkuk, "For the revelation awaits an appointed time; it speaks of the end and will not prove false. Though it linger, wait for it; it will certainly come and will not delay."

What "revelation"? The revelation of God's intents and purposes. Earlier on in the first chapter, the Lord even warns Habakkuk, saying, "For I am going to do something in your days that you would not believe, even if you were told" (v. 5). The Lord in essence was saying, "You are just not going to believe how I am going to work this out—it will seem impossible to you. But remember, I am God; my ways are not your ways. What doesn't make sense to you makes perfect sense to me." Did Habakkuk rest patiently in this? You bet he did! The entire last chapter is dedicated to praising God for His absolute and perfect magnificence.

We, too, can wait expectantly for divine revelation. As a matter of fact, Proverbs 29:18 warns, "Where there is no revelation, the people cast off restraint." If we don't have divine revelation or vision, we become complacent.

Can you think of a time in your life when you were waiting for a divine revelation? Maybe you were praying about switching jobs, or perhaps you were walking excruciatingly slowly through infertility, or maybe the wait to know if you were to marry—ever—seemed endless. All are serious times of waiting for God to reveal His plan and vision for your life. Did discouragement ever creep in? Of course it did. Maybe it's still constantly in your shadow. Did you, and maybe you still do, feel like giving up? Quite likely, yes. These are all examples of complete and total soul- and God-searching. But that's the key to true knowledge.

Soul-searching brings us directly back to seeking God's wisdom and knowledge. Just as the life cycle of just about anything can be diagrammed in a circle, so, too, can our pursuit of God knowledge and wisdom take us on a constantly rotating circle. The stops along the way of a desire to be more Christlike, follow God's directives, find His wisdom and will, and then gain confidence in each of these, will always return us to the beginning (indeed, to the Illustrator) of the circle—God himself. With each trip around this circle, we gain insights and, yes, the knowledge of who God is, to prepare us for the next hike around.

Stillness in Action

As we've seen in the preceding chapter, discernment is a God-given, heightened awareness. You can increase your ability to be aware by the practice of using your senses. Though discernment is spiritual and your senses are physical, you can use your senses to gain an enhanced view of God himself through the nature He created. Use your observation skills to document the characteristics you know of God as being evident in the natural world around you. Take your Bible and journal, hide away from the noise around you, and page through the Psalms. Write down or sketch out the parallels between who God is and what He created. For example, if you can see mountains, write down the characteristics that God and a mountain share (e.g., solid, impenetrable, towering, permanent). Use all your senses: see the birds in the air; smell the earth, the flowers; hear the breeze, the birdsong; touch leaves, seeds, brook water; chew on a blade of grass or a mint leaf.

MEMORY VERSE

"But let him who boasts boast about this: that he understands and knows me, that I am the Lord, who exercises kindness, justice and righteousness on earth, for in these I delight."

JEREMIAH 9:24

PART THREE

I Am God

CHAPTER TEN

"God said to Moses, 'I AM WHO I AM.
This is what you are to say to the Israelites:
I AM has sent me to you.'"

EXODUS 3:14

If you were to finish the sentence "I am ...," how would
you fill in the blank? What words would you use to describe yourself?
Wife, mother, Christian, teacher, politician, nurse, lawyer, writer? I can
think of several words to describe who I am, what my roles are in life,
what my spiritual passion is, where my spiritual gifts are used, even
how my husband and children view me. I could probably carry on for
some length describing myself—as likely you could, too.

However, all of my self-professed qualities are based on my
past—what I've studied, what I've learned, how I've dealt with situations, and the innate nature God put in me. That's how we all are
made up. Mostly based on the past. Even genetically speaking, our
DNA codes are similar to those of our ancestors. And though what
we've experienced in the past may be preparing us for the future,

we haven't arrived there yet, so we can't base our personal qualities on what *might* transpire, only on what *has* transpired.

Why am I bringing this up? When God says, "I AM," He means past, present, and future. As Revelation 1:8 reminds us, " 'I am the Alpha and the Omega,' says the Lord God, 'who is, and who was, and who is to come, the Almighty.' " We can't base our understanding of what God means when He says "I AM" on the same criteria that we base our own words "I am . . ." Tony Evans says, "We are linear, successive creatures, but that is irrelevant to God. He knows about history because He's the God of history, but history doesn't control Him. . . . That verb *AM* is very important because it means that God forever lives in the present tense."[1] The word "am" is a "state of being" verb. That's just what God is all the time—He is a perpetual state of Being.

Isaiah 46:9–10 confirms this, saying, "I am God, and there is no other; I am God, and there is none like me. I make known the end from the beginning, from ancient times, what is still to come. I say: My purpose will stand, and I will do all that I please." Jeremiah 10:10 puts it this way and leaves no room for conjecture: "But the Lord is the true God; he is the living God, the eternal King."

His deity, this indisputable "godhood" (as *Webster's* defines it), is unalterable. His deity is all the characteristics, virtues, ways, knowledge, wisdom, names, etc., that make God who He is. They are complete, comprehensive, perfect, and undeniable. The only variation in God is how *we* as individuals view His deity.

SAME DEITY—DIFFERENT PERCEPTIONS

God always has been, always will be, and doesn't change. His character doesn't change, His qualities don't change. I love the seventeenth verse of James 3. The virtuous qualities listed are what we should strive for. These mirror a reflection of God, since, for us, they come from the wisdom of knowing God. "But the wisdom that comes from heaven is first of all pure; then peace-loving, considerate, submissive, full of mercy and good fruit, impartial and sincere." Jesus displayed each one of these attributes as He ministered on earth (the word "submission" could be applied to Jesus' submitting to death on the cross as God's will). God is every one of these distinctions and more! R. C. Sproul, noted author and speaker, states that God is immutable (unchangeable). But man is mutable. Not only does God not change—He is incapable of change. Man, on the other hand, is not only capable of change, he is designed to change. Because God is perfect, there never has been nor ever will be a need for Him to change, yet He created us to be changeable.

What does change is our *perception* of God. Perhaps you grew up with a view of God as a superior Being who orchestrated life from His easy chair in heaven. Maybe your early teachings inclined you to see Him as unapproachable.

I know my view of Him changed tremendously after I was liberated from a restrictive religious high school. While attending this school, guilt and my utter unworthiness motivated every thought I had and every move I made. I never felt completely forgiven for my sins; indeed, the instructors reminded the students—it seemed at every chance possible—about how deviant we each were. Notorious for "altar calls," the school invited students forward to "prevent an untimely death and therefore a sure damnation in hell." I crept forward, at *every* altar call, fearful and trembling, always thinking, "Maybe I'll get it right this time. Maybe I'll feel forgiven this time." But it never seemed to "work." I'd find myself walking back to the altar week after week, my footfalls as hollow as my heart felt, reconfessing over and over.

This guilt stayed with me even after I left the school at the end of my sophomore year (my parents wisely saw my self-esteem plummeting and knew I needed a new environment). My freedom from this fear of hell and guilt-motivated actions came only as my perception of God changed. Entrenched in a loving church, studying the Bible for God's words of love, and most importantly, forgiving myself, I began to see God in a much broader context. Instead of seeing only

His finger pointed to the pit of hell, I saw His arms outstretched to hold me close. Instead of hearing a stern voice telling me how wretched I behaved, I heard, "I forgive you, I love you, come to me." I found He was a loving God, ready to forgive, not condemn. He didn't want me to go to hell any more than I wanted to, and furthermore, my sins were paid for by Christ the *first* time I asked for forgiveness. How much emotional and spiritual energy I had wasted dragging myself and my guilt to the school church altar week after week!

Freedom from misperceptions of who God is and how He acts for our benefit is so essential to enable us to "be still" before Him. If we don't have confidence in His forgiveness and therefore our worthiness in His sight, then we can't rest quietly in His presence. If we don't understand and wholeheartedly embrace the character traits of God, we are little more than an abused child in the presence of his abuser, wary of the next strike. Is that the view God wants us to have of Him? I think not. Kay Arthur puts it this way: "I believe that every problem in our lives can be traced back to an inadequate or incorrect knowledge of God, or a lack of faith and trust in His person and His ways."[2] If we don't trust His character—the traits that make Him the good, unchanging, and forgiving God—then we can't truly have confidence enough to be still, allowing Him to be God.

SAME DEITY—DIFFERENT NAMES

Though God's character doesn't change, His names reflect how He is ministering in a given situation. Once again, the Bible uses analogies that we can understand to describe His abilities. He doesn't need comparative thinking to understand or describe himself! No, it's our finiteness and limited perception that require Him to use visual imagery that we can understand. Hence the words such as "potter" (Jeremiah 18:1–6) and "craftsman" (Proverbs 8:30). Indeed, just about every task (of the positive nature) we have here on earth can be likened to God's job detail. (Think hard on that one—He is our entire spiritual judicial system, He is our health care system, He is our waste collector, our accountant, our complete educational system—need I go on?)

In Isaiah 9:6 the prophet tells us a few names of the coming Messiah Jesus: "Wonderful Counselor, Mighty God, Everlasting Father, Prince of Peace." And in 44:6: "Israel's King and Redeemer, the Lord Almighty: I am the first and I am the last; apart from me there is no God."

You could page through the Bible and pick out any number of names for God—names He has applied to himself through His inspired Word. Each book of the Bible reminds us of a different characteristic or name that tells us more about the nature of God.

Several years ago my church choir performed the musical production *God With Us.* One portion of the performance is a narration of the books of the Bible and who God reveals himself to be in each book. In other words, He is personified in all the actions documented in the Bible. He's not only *present,* but *represented.* I remember listening to this narration with tears streaming down my face. The parallels between life and God seemed suddenly so obvious to me. Never before had I experienced the significance of the magnitude of the Lord. I felt unworthy and profoundly grateful at the same time. That He would choose me to be a living part of His testimony as evidenced by the Bible suddenly made my relationship with Him so much more personal.

Read for yourself this poignant reminder of God's identity in everything:

"Name Above All Names"

In GENESIS Jesus is the Ram at Abraham's altar.

In EXODUS He's the Passover Lamb.

In LEVITICUS He's the High Priest.

In NUMBERS He's the Cloud by day and Pillar of Fire by night.

In DEUTERONOMY He's the City of our refuge.

In JOSHUA He's the Scarlet Thread out Rahab's window.

In JUDGES He's our Judge.

In RUTH He is our Kinsman Redeemer.

In 1st and 2nd SAMUEL He's our Trusted Prophet.

And in KINGS and CHRONICLES He's our Reigning King.

In EZRA He is our Faithful Scribe.

In NEHEMIAH He's the Rebuilder of everything that is broken.

And in ESTHER He is the Mordecai sitting faithful at the gate.

In JOB He's our Redeemer that ever liveth.

In PSALMS He is my Shepherd and I shall not want.

In PROVERBS and ECCLESIASTES He's our Wisdom.

And in SONG OF SOLOMON He's the Beautiful Bridegroom.

In ISAIAH He's the Suffering Servant.

In JEREMIAH and LAMENTATIONS it is Jesus that is the Weeping Prophet.

In EZEKIEL He's the Wonderful Four-faced Man.

And in DANIEL He is the Fourth Man in the midst of a fiery furnace.

In HOSEA He is my Love that is forever faithful.

In JOEL He baptizes us with the Holy Spirit.

In AMOS He's our Burden Bearer.

In OBADIAH our Savior.

And in JONAH He is the Great Foreign Missionary that takes the Word of God into all of the world.

You go on and see in MICAH He is the messenger with beautiful feet.

In NAHUM He is the Avenger.

In HABAKKUK He is the Lord mighty to save.

In HAGGAI He is the Restorer of our lost heritage.

In ZECHARIAH He is our Fountain.

And in MALACHI He is the Son of Righteousness with healing in His wings.

In MATTHEW Thou art the Christ, the Son of the Living God.

In MARK He is the Miracle Worker.

In LUKE He's the Son of Man.

And in JOHN He is the Door by which every one of us must enter.

In ACTS He is the Shining Light that appears to Saul on the road to Damascus.

In ROMANS He is our Justifier.

In 1st CORINTHIANS our Resurrection.

In 2nd CORINTHIANS our Sin Bearer.

In GALATIANS He redeems us from the law.

In EPHESIANS He is our Unsearchable Riches.

In PHILIPPIANS He supplies our every need.

And in COLOSSIANS He's the Fullness of the Godhead Bodily.

In 1st and 2nd THESSALONIANS He is our Soon Coming King.

In 1st and 2nd TIMOTHY He is the Mediator between God and man.

In TITUS He is our Blessed Hope.

In PHILEMON He is a Friend that sticks closer than a brother.

And in HEBREWS He's the Blood of the everlasting covenant.

In JAMES it is the Lord that heals the sick.

In 1st and 2nd PETER He is the Chief Shepherd.

In 1st, 2nd, and 3rd JOHN it is Jesus who has the tenderness of love.

In JUDE He is the Lord coming with 10,000 saints.

And in REVELATION, lift up your eyes, Church, for your redemption draweth nigh, He is King of kings and Lord of lords.[3]

When put into this context, doesn't the magnificence of God—from the "tenderness" in the three books of John to the "High Priest" in Leviticus—feel reassuring? He is the only Source to meet all of our needs all of the time! I can rest and be still in that knowledge, and so can you!

SAME DEITY—DIFFERENT LANGUAGES

The Great I Am determines who each of us is. As we considered in the first part of this book, He created us as individuals—unique from one another right down to our specific genetic makeup.

I love how we are all different, yet relational with people who are so opposite from ourselves. My husband and I are classic opposites. He's an effervescent extrovert. I'm a shy introvert. He loves crowds, I love solitude. Even my closest friends are different from me and from one another. Some are compulsive neat-nicks, some are completely disorganized (I'm somewhere in the middle).

Along with these personal distinctions, God created in each of us personal languages. Gary Smalley coined the "Language of Love" series. This is basically how we receive and communicate love. Our personal language is how we hear, interpret, respond to, and transmit different types of communication—written, spoken, or creative. Do we *hear* love communicated through words or actions? Do we *respond* through words or actions? When we want to communicate love (or any other emotion) to another person, do we *transmit* through words or actions?

There's a similar pattern in how the Lord speaks to us. These are the languages He uses to speak to us as individuals according to how we're programmed (or created) to hear Him. These languages are how you are tuned in to the whispers of God. Does your personal tuning fork catch a pitch through words? Perhaps you can best hear God's tune through actual events or people. Maybe the notes He uses to capture your attention are through the creative arts. This is your individual "God language"—the way you "hear" God.

One of my strong convictions about women is that we are innately sensitive and finely tuned to the extraneous around us. Of course, in learning to be still before God, this can be beneficial or detrimental. Beneficial because our acute senses enable us to be keenly aware of the presence of God; detrimental because sometimes we have a difficult time filtering distracting interferences (did I just hear spiritual

ADD again?). This God-given, female-heightened awareness is a pure gift from the Lord—it is every woman's birthright. When we use our sensual nature fully—all five physical senses and our spiritual discernment—we hear His voice more distinctly. Perhaps He'll speak to you through something you hear, or call you softly by something you touch, or reach you through something you see. It doesn't matter so much *how* you hear Him, but that you are *expecting* to hear Him.

Can we *expect* to hear God, or is that being presumptuous? Certainly not! He wants to communicate with us; He designed us as relational beings. I find it interesting that one of the first commands the Lord issued to Adam was to name the animals in the Garden of Eden (Genesis 2:19–20). What is required to name anything? Language! Adam and Eve probably cultivated a spoken and symbolic language—the very foundation upon which the rest of human language has developed.

Naturally, the way God communicates with us isn't by voice—His language is different than ours. And we can and should look for ways that He is communicating with us. Let me explain.

Pre-retirement, my parents took up bicycle riding as a form of exercise and companionship. They map out extended trips and pull a trailer behind their truck, bikes strapped on the back, in search of new places to ride and explore. Each morning before they start their daily bike ride, they pray that the Lord will reveal himself to them as they ride. They call this finding God's "fingerprints." They ride attuned, expecting to see an illustration of God's love, faithfulness, or characteristics along their path. And each day God is faithful. My mom says there is one caveat: you do have to keep an eye aware for the signs from God of His presence. But He always shows himself in a very real way to both of them. From the shadows of overhead trees forming a cross on the road, to friendly strangers directing them on the right route, to sightings of young wild animals being protected by their mothers, to brilliant sunrises and sunsets.

You, too, can ask and expect to hear God communicating with

you. Perhaps oversimplifying things, we can divide God's language to us into two general areas of how we'll best hear Him: rationally or viscerally. You may hear Him a little by both means or exclusively by one or the other. The point is to identify your personal hearing aid that picks up God's voice.

RATIONAL HEARING

When you're a rational listener, you likely hear God speaking to you the most through concrete means. You find yourself moved by written or spoken words. A preacher delivers a powerful message and you can feel the Lord speaking directly to your heart through the minister's words. Or maybe written language is the direct route to your heart. The words in a book or the Bible pierce your conscience and you take the meaning very literally. Words, written or spoken, make so much sense to you because you think sensibly and logically.

Rational listeners also see the parallels between the nature of God and the God of nature. You see His reflection in the natural world— a growing vine reminds you of Scripture (John 15:5–6); a tranquil lake reminds you of His peacefulness; a nest of hatchlings reminds you that not one of them will fall without the Lord knowing about it.

I'm somewhat of a rational listener. I like to seek out the Lord's voice through these means. Nature makes the Lord very real to me. I find myself imagining living in Eden, where each tree, shrub, flower, and blade of grass was formed by the tender brush of God's hand. Written words also minister to me. Pages in my favorite books, including my Bible, are earmarked, highlighted, starred, and circled where the words have held me captive to a truth about God.

Maybe you have these traits but can hear the Lord in more subtle ways, too. Perhaps, like me, you're also a visceral listener.

VISCERAL HEARING

If God created you as a visceral listener, you hear Him by more abstract means. You hear the Lord and feel His presence the most through the performing arts, artwork, and dreams.

Drama and music touch you deeply—so deeply you find yourself crying over stanzas of songs or even the melody of particularly dramatic music. Music is imperative to your lifestyle—you play it constantly at home, in the car, and at work. It soothes you, inspires you, and captures you.

Art also speaks to visceral listeners. Intuitively you know what an artist is communicating in a picture. This may be particularly true of artwork about the Lord—blatantly, such as three crosses on a hill, or subtly, as in sheep resting quietly in a pasture. These instinctively touch you with a spiritual truth.

Artwork also sparks an emotional response. A very dear friend of mine is an artist. Her wood-block prints and oil paintings have won multiple awards and sell for thousands of dollars. Many of her paintings depict sheep grazing or lying down. She has spoken frequently of how humbled she feels when someone approaches her and remarks that her art has made the observer weep. Sometimes they can't even articulate exactly what it is about the picture that causes such an emotional response—they just feel deeply touched by the image of resting sheep. Some of us were created with the gift of artistic interpretation.

Visceral listeners also may hear the Lord the most through dreams or visions. The Lord sometimes uses abstract thoughts in the depths of sleep to speak to an insightful thinker. I am a heavy dreamer. My husband tells me I mutter in my dreams, too. Though most of my dreams are inconsequential, occasionally I'll have a dream that is undoubtedly divinely inspired.

One such dream took place years ago, shortly after Peter and I married. We had been invited to a party at the house of a friend of mine from school. There would be people there I hadn't seen in years—some of whom I didn't particularly want to see. As far as I knew, none were Christians. We hadn't really made up our minds about going, but one night about a week before the party, I dreamed that we went to the party and I walked in the front door with my

Bible tucked under my arm. In my dream, we moved from room to room, the whole time my Bible conspicuous under my arm. A simple dream, but a very powerful voice from the Lord telling me we should go to the party and be prepared with His Word. We did go, and an opportunity (not by any means a coincidence) arose for me to talk about the gospel and Christianity with an old boyfriend. If not for that simple Bible-carrying dream, we likely wouldn't have gone. But that's how the Lord spoke to me for His purpose.

How about you? In what language does God reveal himself or speak to you? Perhaps, like me, you're a combination of both. Maybe you've heard the Lord at one time or another through every one of the means I have listed. Terrific! You're highly in tune with God's different languages. But don't feel left out if you haven't yet developed a variety of ears for God's voice. Just as my parents ask to see God's fingerprints, you, too, can ask for Him to reveal himself to you in a way that you'll hear Him. Just remember, you have to stay sharp—keep all your senses open to hearing Him.

When you are confident in how you hear God's personal language to you, you can feel assured in not "missing" His voice. If you hear Him the best through spoken or written words, you'll know not to put forth a lot of effort in trying to hear Him through art. Remember, we're all different, so if a friend hears a song and feels moved, but the feeling eludes you, it doesn't mean the Lord isn't speaking to you; it probably means He uses a different language to communicate with you.

Distinguishing your style of hearing Him is part of who God created you to be. The great I Am will come to meet you at this point of your hearing and interpreting ability. Once again, all you need to do is rest confidently in this knowledge and be still, expecting Him to reveal himself, His characteristics, and His names through the language He created you to hear.

Stillness in Action

I'm going to ask you to once again use all of your senses for this activity. In your journal, list a name or characteristic of God, starting with the letter A and going through the alphabet to Z. Why use your senses for this? Try to think of words that inspire a taste, or a tactile feeling, or a sound. I'll give you an example: A=Approachable (can you hear feet pattering to reach Him?).

B=Bread of Life (that sustains us and satisfies us).

Have fun.

This is a hard but worthwhile exercise.

Try including your children or friends.

MEMORY VERSE

"The heavens declare the glory of God; the skies proclaim the work of his hands. Day after day they pour forth speech; night after night they display knowledge. There is no speech or language where their voice is not heard."

PSALM 19:1-2

CHAPTER ELEVEN

God

"Yet for us there is but one God, the Father,
from whom all things came and for whom
we live; and there is but one Lord, Jesus Christ,
through whom all things came
and through whom we live."

1 CORINTHIANS 8:6

Imagine for a moment that you are pregnant with triplets. Even before you knew you had conceived, the minuscule zygote split into three equal parts—forming three identical cell masses. As the babies grow into life-forms, their genetic makeup will be exactly the same. They are destined to have the same hair color, the same eyes, the same blood type, and even, as they mature outside the womb, the same likes and dislikes.

In a simplistic way this is similar to the unexplainable spiritual Trinity. Three in One. God the Father, God the Son, and God the Spirit. Why a caveat of "unexplainable"? Because we can't comprehend three separate functioning identities in one body. Some have likened the Trinity to water, as it has one component but three separate forms: liquid, ice, and steam. Or the Trinity could be compared to an egg: shell, white, and yolk—separate identities, but all part of one egg.

The doctrine of the Trinity is one of those things that keeps us on our toes; it requires trust and faith. It requires that we abandon our quest for complete knowledge about God (the desire for a pure and full knowledge of God led Adam and Eve into permanent exile). Again, we wouldn't have a need for God if we had Him all figured out.

A desire to understand the Trinity does lead to a huge respect for God, however. We can't help but honor Him and hold Him in high esteem. How can we not, when we realize that even with all the imagination He invested in our brains, we still can't fathom Him? Despite all the human knowledge He has granted us, from telescopes that peer into deep space, to medical technology, to computers that can outsmart us, He still puts limits on our comprehension of Him. Just as Tony Evans' book title declares, *Our God Is Awesome!*

If our God is that great, He has certainly garnered my respect! How about yours?

LOVE, HONOR, AND RESPECT

I remember my wedding day. A beautiful, clear, breezy day in mid-June greeted Peter and me with our guests. My bridesmaids and I ate an early morning breakfast of toast and eggs—and I felt sick for the rest of the day. I remember acting particularly cranky about the photos taken at my parents' house before the ceremony—it was *my* day and *I* wanted everything perfect! For the most part, I remember it all vividly (it helps that we have a video recording of the ceremony), the good and the not-so-good.

As I walked down the aisle, my arm crooked tightly in my father's, my stomach felt hot and knotted. What was I doing, an intensely private person, about to profess my lifelong love to Peter in front of 150 people? After all, I was only twenty—how could I be committing my entire life to this cute blond man standing before

me? Did I even know what "forever" meant? Emotion so over-
whelmed me, I did what came naturally to me. I cried. Through the
entire ceremony, I wept. On the videotape, taken from the balcony
behind me, you can see my maid of honor repeatedly handing me
tissues. At one point my two sisters, standing up front with me,
started crying, too, and all of our shoulders began shaking uncon-
trollably. The pastor wisely inserted an unplanned prayer to help us
try to regain our composure.

That's about all I remember of the ceremony itself. I don't recall
what the pastor said; I don't remember my mother and father saying
they would entrust me to Peter; I don't remember saying our vows.
My nerves and emotions cut off my memory of those particulars.

Partly because we have evidence on the video that I did indeed
say the vows, and partly because Peter remembers me saying them,
I have confidence that I did actually repeat the important words to
love, honor, cherish, and obey Peter for the rest of my life. (That
doesn't seem so daunting anymore—I adore him more now than I
did then.)

Why am I bringing up my wedding? I can see why in the gospel
of John, Jesus compares our relationship in the church as a marriage
to Him (3:28–30). This lifelong, permanent, honoring relationship
He desires us to have with Him is just like the vows we say at our
wedding. And yes, there is fear and trepidation involved in this intensely private yet immensely public union. *Obey?* Won't I lose my
free will? *Honor?* Will I lose my individuality? *In sickness and in
health?* Regardless of whether I feel happy or not? *Forever?* There's
no way out?

As frighteningly restrictive as this may sound, we actually find
freedom in our spiritual marriage to Christ. We desire this intense
union with Him because the benefit is all ours. He holds us in high
esteem—as a bridegroom ought to hold his bride. He honors us so
much that He laid down His life for us—as we in our marriage ought
to be willing to die for our loved one. God's personal relationship

with us through Christ is the model for our marriage.

Just as I love, honor, respect, and obey my husband, so, too, is my relationship with God. The Lord doesn't demand this of me—He asks it of me. I gave this devotion wholeheartedly when I committed my life to Him. This is why it's my personal conviction that a public profession of faith—either through adult baptism or an altar call commitment—is a necessary step in the salvation process. Just as a woman stands in front of a crowd to profess her undying love to her husband, she needs to publicly declare her permanent commitment to God.

This shows honor to God and respect for His awesomeness. Our honor and respect give Him great pleasure. Isaiah 62:5 says, "As a bridegroom rejoices over his bride, so will your God rejoice over you." Actually, I feel completely humbled that He would even want me as His bride. But He does. Not only does He want me as His love, He makes me feel so clean and free of defilement in my life that I can be clothed in white in His presence.

Even while feeling humbled, I feel honored. I can feel confident that He has indeed chosen me to be part of His heavenly wedding party. In this place of feeling honored, I again return that emotion to Him, to encompass Him. I look at it as a revolving circle of cherishing. He cherishes me as a groom treasures his new wife, and I want to do the same for Him. I honor Him. I respect Him. I want to please Him.

Do you know what this mutual cherishing leads to? You guessed it! An ability to be still in His presence. I don't need to strive for His love and acceptance, it's already there. I don't need to "accomplish" anything, He loves me regardless. I can sit quietly at His feet, and His love for me will always be my veil.

For several months after our wedding ceremony, I made Peter fresh bran or blueberry muffins for breakfast. Though I'd never discussed it with him, I thought this was the standard by which he would measure my worthiness as a wife. After about six months, he sheepishly asked if we could have something *different* for breakfast. I responded, "Of course, but I thought muffins were what you wanted. I was just trying to make you happy."

He smiled and said, "You don't have to *do* or *cook* anything for me to make me happy. I'm just as happy eating cereal—as long as I'm with you."

"Oh."

It's the same in our relationship with God. We don't have to *do* anything to make Him love us or cherish us. He does that automatically, regardless of our efforts or worthiness. His greater desire is for us to simply be in communion with Him. Any *doing* for Him should be born of our desire to serve Him—not out of an obligation to perform for Him.

Trying to do for God, or attempting to win His approval, leads me to believe that our actions aren't motivated by honor, love, and respect, but by fear. In the marriage relationship, do the bride and groom marry out of fear of each other? I hope not! Certainly it's love that has brought them to the point of pledging their undying commitment.

I'm very aware that there may be readers who are in abusive relationships right now, and fear is the motivation in their lives. If this is the case for you, I recognize it's difficult for you to understand a comparison between your union with God and your union with an unloving, abusive spouse. But if you can look at it from a heavenly perspective, that God's side of the marriage union with us is perfect, then perhaps you can find your relationship with the Lord to be motivated by pure love, not fear. An abusive, manipulative marriage relationship (or any abusive relationship for that matter) is not a healthy relationship. Do not compare the patterns of this type of relationship with how God desires to be connected with us.

He does not expect or want fear and trembling in response to His reaching out to us. And though He wants respect, He doesn't demand it. What does the Bible mean when it says we are to "fear the Lord"? Let's take a look at it.

THE FEAR OF THE LORD

God is certainly a fear-inspiring power. God certainly has proven He has the capability to create and destroy in the same breath. God certainly can and will continue to do what His plan has ordained from the beginning of time. These indisputable truths make us realize our limitations. So, if we have respect for God, do we also fear what God can do? Yes and no.

If we are blatantly and defiantly participating in sinful acts, then, yes, I think we might want to glance over our shoulder for the inevitable consequences of our sinful choices. But is God out to get us? Is He waiting on His all-powerful throne in heaven for us to slip up so He can administer judgment on us? I don't think so. Yes, He'll correct us as a parent corrects a wayward child. Yes, He'll allow difficulties in our lives to draw us closer to Him. Yes, it will seem that people around us are not receiving their due. But is He waiting with a strike of lightning at His fingertips to destroy us? No.

He is an all-powerful, all-loving God. His power is beyond what we can comprehend, and His love is beyond anything we'll ever experience here on earth. He desires to give us the benefit of His unfathomable, immeasurable love. He has already proved this: "For God so loved the world that he gave his one and only Son" (John 3:16). That's love—not fear-producing wrath.

So why should we "fear the Lord"? If all He truly wants is to love us and to do what's best for us, we don't need to be afraid, do we? Exactly. We don't.

WHAT, THEN, IS "GOD FEAR"?

Most of the Scriptures citing "fear of the Lord" either begin or end with a condition, caveat, or equation about "God fear." The Proverbs probably hold the most "fear the Lord" commands: "The fear of the Lord is the beginning of knowledge" (1:7). "The fear of the Lord is the beginning of wisdom" (9:10). In other words, we show some intelligence by having respect for God.

One of my language teachers in high school always reminded us that the word "is" can be substituted with the word "equals." Proverbs 8:13 says, "To fear the Lord [equals] to hate evil." So a good description of the fear of the Lord is how we respond to evil. If we love, honor, respect, and hold God in high esteem (i.e., fear Him), we will, of course, dislike anything evil, because evil is the antithesis of God.

I like the promise of Proverbs 19:23: "The fear of the Lord leads to life: Then one rests content, untouched by trouble." Showing God the respect He deserves gives us rest and contentment! And as we learned in an earlier chapter, inner contentment diffuses the frenetic pace of our lives.

It is important to note that the fear the Bible speaks of in reference to the Lord is not the same as the common fears of heights or water or flying. Those fears invoke a physiological response in our bodies. It's called the "fight or flight" response. When we are afraid of something, our instinct is to put up a nasty fight—hitting, punching, kicking, etc.—or to simply run away as fast as we can. As we have seen, this is not the response God is looking for when we come to Him. He wants our respect, our honor, our awe in His presence.

When Peter and I met on a college-sponsored European study trip, we took to hiking around the outskirts of the towns we visited. It was a cheap and fun way to explore places, and we had wonderful conversations that eventually led to our feelings of love for each other. One such hike I'll forever remember distinctly. A campground we stayed at in a small town in Germany was based in the shadow of a large foothill. Peter and I decided to climb it one afternoon. Not finding a clear path anywhere, we just started bushwhacking our way up. (Okay, call it the stupidity of youth.) It proved to be a tough climb. Hand over hand at some points, we pulled ourselves toward the top. About halfway up we came across the carcass of a deer, one front leg at a grotesque angle hanging below its knee. The pitiful thing looked as though it had tried to run down the steep hill and broke a leg in its flight. If a nimble deer could fall, break apart, and die so easily on this semi-mountain, I knew I sure didn't want to attempt to go back down.

Though the climb grew more difficult, we persevered until near the top we came across a chain link fence. The fence surrounded a home complex: a house, garage, a few other outbuildings, and a pool. But what really caught our eyes was a paved driveway on the other side of the complex. A way out from the near jungle we'd just come through! We scampered over the fence and started walking toward where the driveway seemed to exit the hillside. We hadn't moved more than several yards when a snarling, barking German shepherd stalked up behind us. I remember turning to Peter and calmly saying, "Don't worry, I can handle this." After all, my family had owned dogs all my life—I wasn't afraid of them. Then the dog started nipping at our heels. The hair stood up on the back of my neck and I bent over to pick up a stick, never taking my eyes off the dog. My voice cracking, I said, "Want to fetch?" The dog was not amused. Turning back to Peter I said, "Run!" And did we run! The dog pursued us, and though I'm sure he could easily have knocked us down or attacked, thankfully, he didn't. We tumbled over the gate at the driveway entrance and slowed to a walk. Eventually our pounding hearts regained a more normal rhythm, and we found our way back to the campground (via a road, I might add).

That kind of true, deep, near-panic fear has only happened to me a few times. My instincts each time have been to run and protect myself. In the nasty dog scenario, did I fear him? You bet. Was I afraid for my life and body? Yes, I was. Did I have a respect for him? Of course. Is this the same fear God produces in me? Thankfully, no. God is approachable. The dog was not. Something threatening to my life is not approachable.

In respecting and fearing the Lord, my respect for God's awesomeness is born of a regard for His "personal space." In the case of the dog, we had violated his personal space; he was only protecting what was his property. Though a comparison of God to an angry dog doesn't nearly do God the justice He deserves, it serves to show us what the Lord means when He calls us to "fear" Him. He wants us to hold Him in high regard. This is the "know that I am God" part of Psalm 46:10. Know enough about Him not to tread on His personal space. Don't try to infringe on His area. Don't try to short-cut across His plan. He's still approachable, He still wants us to come to Him with everything in our lives, but we cannot and should not try to find a path across His territory without His assistance. It is, again, letting God be God of His domain—which is everything.

Genesis 3:23 says that the Lord banished Adam and Eve from the Garden of Eden for their willful disobedience. Verse 24 speaks of God protecting His domain: "After he drove the man out, he placed on the east side of the Garden of Eden cherubim and a flaming sword flashing back and forth to guard the way to the tree of life." In other words, the garden was now off limits. A flaming, flashing sword would guard the perfect garden of God for eternity. There is still evidence of that flaming sword in our lives. It's a cautionary sign, a "go slow" feeling, a warning of danger ahead. It's that nudge of the Holy Spirit in our inner quiet if we even think of defiantly treading on God's toes.

WHAT ABOUT OUR HUMAN FEARS?

God wants us to approach Him. Freedom to seek out the guidance and love of God in His domain is verified in Romans 8:39: "Neither height nor depth, nor anything else in all creation, will be able to separate us from the love of God that is in Christ Jesus our

Lord." When we are afraid, God actually wants us to run *to* Him, not *from* Him. As it says in Isaiah 41:10, "So do not fear, for I am with you; do not be dismayed, for I am your God. I will strengthen you and help you; I will uphold you with my righteous right hand." In other words, He will take our hands and guide us across the terrifying places.

I love Psalm 46 in its entirety (and obviously the tenth verse in particular). This is such a poignant reminder of God's powerfulness and how, regardless of what is happening around us, He is in charge:

> God is our refuge and strength, an ever-present help in trouble. Therefore we will not fear, though the earth give way and the mountains fall into the heart of the sea, though its waters roar and foam and the mountains quake with their surging. There is a river whose streams make glad the city of God, the holy place where the Most High dwells. God is within her, she will not fall; God will help her at break of day. Nations are in uproar, kingdoms fall; he lifts his voice, the earth melts.

Wow. Various natural calamities are spoken of here, yet the Psalm starts with His promises, saying in essence that these promises will hold true through all of these potential disasters. I can't help but think of the houses built on the coastline all along the eastern and western seaboards. Because of erosion, these homes—some with multimillion-dollar price tags—are literally dropping into the sea.

Was this Psalm written for them, too? Absolutely. And every other part of the world that experiences flooding, earthquakes, volcanic eruptions, etc. Could David have known when he wrote this Psalm of the incidence of these disasters in the thousands of years to come? He could not have personally known what we needed to hear in the twentieth century, but since all Scripture is inspired by God himself, the Lord put the words in David's heart.

David's world experience was comparatively limited when he wrote his psalms. During the years of David's prolific poetry, few seamen had explored past the Mediterranean. They thought the world ended at the Straits of Gibraltar where the Rock of Gibraltar to the northeast and the Atlas Mountains in Africa to the southwest formed the "Gates of Hell." The few who had the courage to explore beyond this point never returned.

Yet when David wrote, he had, as it were, a complete worldview. The Lord entrusted immense faith and vision to David. There is no way he could have written what he did without God giving him some sort of knowledge of the immensity of creation—as evidenced in so many of the Psalms.

We might even conclude that the Psalms were written specifically for the far-off generations to come after David. The Lord knew then that we would need His assurance now when so much calamity and disaster and tragedy falls around us daily.

But mind-numbing, panic-driven, incapacitating fear is not born of God. I wish I could answer the "why's" of this world. Why is there starvation? Why is there abuse? Why is there war? Why do people die in floods, earthquakes, volcanic eruptions, and tidal waves? All I know is that there is a far bigger question that God is answering when these things happen.

Ecclesiastes asks some of these soul-searching questions, concluding that all of our efforts or attempts to understand are simply "chasing after the wind." I love that expression. Wind ruffles, destroys, or brings relief. But it can't be captured or held hostage.

So, too, is asking "why?" or living in fear of calamity. It's chasing after the wind. There is no way to predict what will happen; there's nothing we can do to change God's design or the pattern of "wind" in our lives. I believe that's why the book of Ecclesiastes ends, after waxing on about the "meaninglessness" of life, with: "Here is the conclusion of the matter: Fear God and keep his commandments, for this is the whole duty of man" (12:13).

It's so simple, and it brings us back to fearing God by respecting and obeying His commands and His plan for our lives.

GOD'S HOLINESS

Without fault. Perfect and pure. Tony Evans defines holiness: "The holiness of God is His intrinsic and transcendent purity, the standard of righteousness to which the whole universe must conform."[1] Evans also says God's holiness is at the center of all of God's characteristics. It's like the hub in the middle of the wheel. All of God's other traits extend from His central holiness, forming a framework of support for all of His attributes.

Divine holiness is the measure by which we can see how unholy we are without Christ. In Him, we have the holiness of God.

HOLY IN HIS DWELLING PLACE

First Kings 3 relays the powerful rise to kinghood of Solomon— even as a child. His father, King David, saw deep potential in Solomon; perhaps he saw a primary wisdom, perhaps he saw a desire to follow the Lord. Regardless of David's motivation, he entrusted his entire kingdom to Solomon's care. It obviously turned out to be the right choice, because Solomon humbly requested of God the only thing he could think of when asked what the Lord could grant him: "Give your servant a discerning heart to govern your people and to distinguish between right and wrong" (1 Kings 3:9). So began Solomon's incredible God-endowed wisdom and wealth. Under his wise reign, a palace was built and a temple erected—no small feat. Both took a total of twenty years to complete. The temple was built to house the ark of the covenant—that precious box containing the original, hand-chiseled Ten Commandments issued to Moses and the Israelites at Mount Sinai in the desert.

Moving the ark to the temple proved a festive time. From far and wide in the nation of Israel, everyone came to witness this historic and symbolic move of the ark to its new and permanent quarters. The inner sanctuary was equipped and designed specifically to accommodate the ark, where no one would be allowed to trespass. Most remarkably, this special chamber, named the "Holy Place," would become an actual dwelling place for God's spirit:

> When the priests withdrew from the Holy Place, the
> cloud filled the temple of the Lord. And the priests could not
> perform their service because of the cloud, for the glory of the
> Lord had filled his temple.
> Then Solomon said, "The Lord has said that he would
> dwell in a dark cloud; I have indeed built a magnificent temple
> for you, a place for you to dwell forever" (1 Kings 8:10–13).

Who among us would have the simultaneously intimate and comprehensive understanding of God's holiness that we would recognize the need and act as a visionary to build a temple and offer a room for His original words and for His Spirit to dwell? Solomon did. After God filled the Holy Place, King Solomon praised the Lord in an eloquent prayer of thanksgiving and blessing. Then for two weeks the entire nation made blood sacrifices and burnt offerings in the Lord's name, offering praise and thanksgiving.

Finally, after everyone had departed for their homes and villages, Solomon (who surely must have been exhausted from all the revelry) had another visit from the Lord. What God says to Solomon touches the very heart of our relationship with Him: " 'I have heard the prayer and plea you have made before me; I have consecrated this temple, which you have built, by putting my Name there forever. *My eyes and my heart will always be there*' " (1 Kings 9:3, italics mine). Why is this so basic to our relationship with God? Because this temple is representative of our bodies in which He now dwells (1 Corinthians 6:19).

It's important to remember that the writing and living of the Old Testament occurred before the arrival of the promised Christ—hence the blood sacrifices prior to Christ's sacrifice and none necessary since. Many of the stories and events of the Old Testament are a preambular representation of what Christ's life and death on earth would accomplish. The Holy Place, built with such painstaking care, is like our spiritual being, which we nourish and build with equally painstaking care. Indeed, our bodies are the Holy Place where God dwells because of Christ's intermediary power on our behalf.

The other part of the Holy Place's significance is the ark itself. The tablets were the written Law of God—the only Law the people had at that point in time. No wonder they couched themselves so rigidly in rituals and ceremonies. They had ten relatively short laws and many practices. By comparison, we have the entire Bible (remember that the New Testament frees us from the ceremonial rituals of the Old Testament). Of course, they were much more dependent on signs, wonders, casting lots, the natural world, prophets, etc., than we are today. We are dependent on the Bible and a personal relationship with Jesus Christ who intervenes for us before the Father.

Does this make us less or more holy than our predecessors? If anything, I believe it makes us less attentive of the need for holy awareness in our lives. In our busyness, our lives have lost touch with "holy" practices because (1) there is now less of a perceived need for them, and (2) because we don't take the time for them.

It's spiritual ADD again, blocking our vision for holiness. If we're so distracted that we're constantly evading, ducking, crouching, leaping, and flinging ourselves through our lives, how can we possibly become aware of God's holiness? A perception of holiness requires quiet. A desire for the ability to recognize God's holiness requires that we be still long enough to dwell on the depth and breadth of what holiness means.

WALKING ON HOLY GROUND

For a number of years Peter's sister, Anita, ran a Children in Worship program at her church. More than a Sunday school time, the goal was to teach children about worshiping the Lord in ways that they found exciting and relevant to their young lives. Before each class the children lined up in the hall outside the classroom and stood mutely waiting for Anita to ask them each the decisive question: "Are you ready for worship?" With a silent nod of the head, each child quietly and respectfully walked into the classroom. Order and respect remained throughout the lessons, week after week. Their consistent attitude of reverence astounded me. As adults we can learn much from the respect and reverence these children displayed for God's "holy ground"—the classroom in which they learned about Him.

I'll be the first to admit to the times I've walked into my church sanctuary thinking about something other than the significance of this room reserved for God's dwelling. I may be replaying a conversation in my mind, or thinking about what I'm going to do when I get home, or talking to my husband or a friend. When I do these things, I am not displaying a "ready to worship" attitude. It's more likely that I am trampling on the holiness of the hour and the place. The church sanctuary is the place where *we've asked* God to meet us. We've invited His presence, but then we ignore the significance of it. A church is the building where we go to set ourselves apart on Sundays to show God the honor and respect due His name. The fourth commandment says, "Remember the Sabbath day by keeping it holy" (Exodus 20:8). That remembrance and honor should begin the second we walk in the front door of the church.

Moses knew what it felt like to tread on God's holy ground (Exodus 3:1–6). The Lord appeared in the form of a burning bush to charge Moses as the advocate to help the Israelites escape from Pharaoh's harsh rule. From verse 5, " 'Do not come any closer,' God said. 'Take off your sandals, for the place where you are standing is holy ground.' " Moses' response was to hide his face in fear, knowing that if he saw God in the burning bush he would die.

Now, let's be honest with ourselves for a minute here. Wouldn't you want a peek, just a glimpse of God if He were right before you in substance? I fear my own human curiosity would get the best of me. I think I'd look. How about you? I think the reason we'd look is because deep inside we don't have a true appreciation of the complete holiness of God; certainly not to the extent that our forefathers did. God's holiness has been diluted by our own unconcentrated lives. The busier we've become in the relentless pursuit of self, the further we've removed ourselves from a deep, abiding conviction of God's holiness.

Isaiah 48:17 reads, "This is what the Lord says—your Redeemer, the Holy One of Israel: I am the Lord your God, who teaches you what is best for you, who directs you in the way you should go." That our holy God wants to be so intimately involved in my life is humbling. The holy God who created everything, who has a finger on the pulse of the entire universe, cares enough about my life to "teach" and "direct" me. This knowledge empowers me to want to be a willing and pliable student. Respect and reverence are, again, the key words in our approach to our relationship with God. Respect for what He is capable of doing (corrections or blessings in our lives), and reverence for all of His care-giving characteristics.

Stillness in Action

"Holy ground" can be any place you've designated as a point where you want to regularly meet with God. It could be your prayer corner, it could be the route you walk every morning for exercise, it could even be your car.

Designate a place for yourself that you decide will be your holy ground. Remind yourself each time you enter this place that you have asked God to meet you here. Spend time quietly waiting for Him to reveal himself to you in a way that you'll "hear" (chapter 10). Record in your journal how His holiness touches you when you are on your chosen holy ground.

MEMORY VERSE

"And now, O Israel, what does the Lord your God ask of you but to fear the Lord your God, to walk in all his ways, to love him, to serve the Lord your God with all your heart and with all your soul, and to observe the Lord's commands and decrees that I am giving you today for your own good?"

DEUTERONOMY 10:12–13

CHAPTER TWELVE

Trusting God to Be God

"Trust in the Lord with all your heart
and lean not on your own understanding;
in all your ways acknowledge him,
and he will make your paths straight."

PROVERBS 3:5–6

One of my multiple mottoes in life is "It's all a matter of choice." In the case of "Be still, and know that I am God," what is the choice? Whether I will trust God or not. Whether I will choose to trust Him in my stillness or choose to run around, frantically trying to control my own life.

Everything we do every day involves choice. We can choose to get out of bed or to stay in bed; we can choose to eat breakfast or to be hungry; we can choose to wear the black dress or the red one. Some of these "choices" might not seem like decisions at all—many of our unconscious decisions every day are just routine activities of daily living. Conscious or not, we make multiple choices every day, some of little consequence, some of enormous consequence.

The book of Joshua tells the story of how the Israelites fight for their Promised Land. They struggle with whom to trust to help them when faced with odds against them in battles. When they trust the Lord, He is faithful to help them—proving over and over His ever-present help. By the end of the book, they are confronted with the decision of whom they will serve forever—themselves and idols, or God. Joshua isn't afraid of convicting them with the hard questions: "But if serving the Lord seems undesirable to you, then choose for yourselves this day whom you will serve" (24:15). Ask yourself the same thing. Whom will I choose to serve? Whom will I choose to trust?

I know I'm not worthy of my own trust. Nor should I put my complete trust in others. My husband deserves and has earned my trust, and many of my friends have proved to be trustworthy with my thoughts or feelings that I've shared. But no one is 100 percent worthy of our complete trust except God himself. One thing I've learned is that humans will disappoint. Because humans are fallible. Other people are not designed to be able to meet all of my needs all of the time. If they were, I wouldn't need God. Numbers 23:19 confirms this, saying, "God is not man, that he should lie, nor a son of man, that he should change his mind. Does he speak and then not act? Does he promise and not fulfill?" Quite simply, no. Indeed, He *does* speak and act, and He *does* promise and fulfill. He is faithful.

GOD IS FAITHFUL

Not only is the Lord worthy of my wholehearted trust, He is wholeheartedly trustworthy. His whole heart is into remaining faithful to me. His faithfulness is not measured by our faith (or lack thereof), thank goodness! His faithfulness is permanent, unchangeable, and complete: "I will make your faithfulness known through all generations . . . you established your faithfulness in heaven itself" (Psalm 89:1–2). And in 2 Timothy 2:13, it says, "If we are faithless, he will remain faithful, for he cannot disown himself." Looking again at Joshua and how God remained faithful to the Israelites,

21:45 says, "Not one of all the Lord's good promises to the house of Israel failed; every one was fulfilled." That's twofold faithfulness. Not only were His promises completed but they stayed sound. How reassuring!

In Exodus 14, after the Israelites were freed with Moses, they suddenly encounter the Egyptians. The terrified Hebrews shout at Moses, "What have you done to us by bringing us out of Egypt?" (v. 11). Moses, despite his earlier professed shortage of words, confronts and comforts them, saying, "Do not be afraid. Stand firm and you will see the deliverance the Lord will bring you today. The Egyptians you see today you will never see again. The Lord will fight for you; *you need only be still*" (vv. 13–14, italics mine).

Now that's faith. An army approaching with nothing but death and retribution on their minds, and Moses says in effect, "Stay where you are, don't move, God will take care of this mess." Then God instructs Moses to tell the Israelites to gather in toward the Red Sea. He does indeed provide a way for them to escape. First, He restores their strength by giving them a night of rest; the Angel of God and a pillar of cloud behind them, preventing any further advance of Pharaoh's army. Then the next day, after resting and waiting on the Lord to provide an out, the Red Sea parted. The Israelites passed through on dry land, and the Egyptians, trying to follow, drowned.

What I find so interesting about this whole miraculous adventure is that Moses had said they would *never* see the same Egyptians again. He was exactly right, because they all perished! So not only were the Israelites saved from the Egyptians, they were never confronted again by the army. That's God's twofold faithfulness again!

Despite these powerful testimonies to God's timeless faithfulness, it's still difficult to quiet ourselves in rapid-fire situations. We need to remember that God deals in the supernatural and we deal in the natural. We just don't see *how* a circumstance can possibly work out because all we have is tangible evidence in front of us—

broken relationships, work-related disappointments, wayward children, etc. But these things do not discourage the Lord. He has proven himself repeatedly faithful in relationships, in His protection, and in His provision.

If I doubt in any area of my life, what does that say about my perception of God? That He's not God? That He doesn't have control? That He doesn't know what's best for me? That He can't or won't take care of me? Pam Farrel asks it this way: "What attribute of God [am I] not believing?"[1]

Am I not trusting His sufficiency? Am I not trusting Him with my children's lives? Am I not trusting Him financially? In answer to these: He may not provide in the way *we* think best. Frequently He'll provide in a way that stretches our faith. An answer to finances might be in the form of a second job in the eleventh hour and fifty-ninth minute. Or, after an extended time away from God's plan, a child might crawl back into His favor—scratched, sore, and bruised from the world. It may seem an eternity to us while we are waiting and praying, but is God less faithful because it took Him longer to bring the child back than we would have liked? No. The bigger answer is there was something to be learned—by all—in the interim.

SURRENDERING TO HIS FAITHFULNESS

In Charles R. Swindoll's book *Intimacy With the Almighty*, he reminds us that allowing God to have control is really the only choice we have if we are to feel any sense of stillness in spirit. He says, "Nothing under His control can ever be out of control." So simple, so profound. He also reveals how giving in to God is actually acting responsibly: "I am finally learning that surrendering to my sovereign Lord, leaving the details of my future in His hands, is the most responsible act of obedience I can do."[2]

Ah, surrender. A word picture comes to mind. I can see myself carrying the heavy burden of all my concerns and frets and worries. I'm valiantly trying to balance all these in my arms and hands and move forward at the same time. But fear is a dense box right at eye level, blocking my sight. Worry about the future of my children pokes under the ribs, and the heaviness of bearing relationships is tiring my shoulders. But what happens when I surrender? I lift my arms in the air—palms open and stretched upward: "I surrender, I surrender!" And what happens to all that stuff I had been hugging to my chest? It drops at my feet. Who's going to sweep up the mess I've created? The Lord. *I willingly surrender then, Lord. You carry this burden—it's too much for me to bear alone.*

I can assure you that He is completely and unerringly trustworthy and faithful to take all that we can't handle when we surrender to Him. But you don't have to trust me on that count—trust Him!

I was sharing with a friend of mine how Tony Evans uses the word picture of our lives as a parade. We just keep walking down the street, and the only perspective we have is what we've just passed and the block we can see in front of us. But it's as if God is in a blimp high above the parade, and He can see the whole path laid out before us.[3] My friend piped up and said, "I also think we presume that because we've been walking the whole time, we're going to keep walking forever. We assume that walking is the only means by which we'll get to where we're going. But God sometimes calls us to use a different means of travel. He might have us ride a bike, or start jogging, or sit in a wheelchair. We can't presume that just because the way we've always done things is the way we will continue to do things."

How right she is! It's scary to think of jumping off the perpetual treadmill of a frenetic life. It's intimidating to think of picking up a new way to travel. I think many women who do take the leap will land a little unsteadily, regain their balance, and promptly question, "Now what do I do?" When you do make the choice to change your lifestyle to embrace stillness, you may find yourself saying, "I don't know how to operate any differently than the status quo of constant motion." But God will meet you with a new mode of transportation. A guaranteed-to-be-slower one.

With this slower way of moving through life, you will be better able to tune in to God's voice. The wind will no longer be whistling distractingly and deafeningly in your ears because of your jet flight through life. Instead, quietness will surround you and you'll be able to hear His voice the first time He speaks, not after He's called your name a dozen times.

TRUSTING HIM WITH YOUR LIFE

For the first couple of years of our marriage, we were the caretakers of a large farm. We loved the open fields, the woodlands, and the yards we tended. But we longed for a place of our own. A place where we could dig as deep as possible or look as high as our eyes could see and call it all home. When we did find our home, it needed so much work that many others couldn't see past the decay and years of reclamation that lay ahead for us. But, being visionaries, we could see what a gorgeous homestead it could become—besides, the price was right. I prayed for confirmation, and it came in the form of Psalm 37, where it says seven times, in various forms, "you will inherit the land." I've often looked back on that Psalm, particularly verses 1–9, as a source of encouragement. A couple of years ago I again sought out those verses and found guide words that I now use as a blueprint for keeping my focus on the Lord.

> *Do not fret* because of evil men or be envious of those who do wrong; for like the grass they will soon wither, like green plants they will soon die away. *Trust* in the Lord and do good; dwell in the land and enjoy safe pasture. *Delight* yourself in the Lord and he will give you the desires of your heart. *Commit* your way to the Lord; trust in him and he will do this: He will make your righteousness shine like the dawn, and the justice of your cause like the noonday sun. *Be still* before the Lord and wait patiently for him; do not fret when men succeed in their ways,

when they carry out their wicked schemes. *Refrain* from anger and *turn* from wrath; do not fret—it leads only to evil. For evil men will be cut off, but those who *hope* in the Lord will inherit the land. (italics mine)

Do not fret
Trust
Delight
Commit
Be still
Refrain
Turn
Hope

These words concisely sum up how we can put being still into action:

- Do not fret: Stop wringing your hands in worry and inattentiveness.
- Trust: God is always faithful.
- Delight: Choose contentment.
- Commit: Use your senses to deepen your relationship with God.
- Be still: Wait expectantly for the Lord.
- Refrain: Stop trying to be God of your own life.
- Turn: Surrender to Him.
- Hope: Know that God's way will always be the best way.

If there is such a thing as a "formula" for the avenue by which we can achieve the attentive relationship God desires us to have with Him, it is this. And nestled in the middle is "Be still."

Are you saying, "I want this!" yet? Do you know where this brings us? Back to the point where it is a choice; a purposeful, conscious decision to *stop* an attention deficit lifestyle. That's what you've been doing through this book. You now have the insights into why we function the way we do (i.e., our humanity). You've learned that stillness is more than a physical quiet, but an inner tranquillity. You now have the tools to build a deeper relationship with God because you've learned about gaining His wisdom and knowledge. And, lastly, you are learning God is worth trusting because of His permanent faithfulness. So now it's just a matter of choosing to act on all this knowledge and change your life!

MAKE A PLAN

First comes the conscious choice to change your life, then comes the decision to trust God with your life, and next comes the practical plan of implementing stillness in your life. You need to make a plan to map out your individual path for gaining stillness.

I'm sure you've been praying for the Lord to grow stillness in your life throughout your reading this book. Continue to pray for your relationship with Him. How does He want to relate to you? How can you eagerly dedicate time to Him? Are there changes He wants you to make in your life? Proverbs 19:21 reminds us, "Many are the plans in a man's heart, but it is the Lord's purpose that prevails." Pray specifically about what "purpose" He has for you, right now, during this time of your life.

Ecclesiastes 3:1–8 says there is a time for everything:

> There is a time for everything, and a season for every activity
> under heaven:
>   a time to be born and a time to die,
>   a time to plant and a time to uproot,
>   a time to kill and a time to heal,
>   a time to tear down and a time to build,
>   a time to weep and a time to laugh,
>   a time to mourn and a time to dance,
>   a time to scatter stones and a time to gather them,
>   a time to embrace and a time to refrain,
>   a time to search and a time to give up,
>   a time to keep and a time to throw away,

> a time to tear and a time to mend,
> a time to be silent and a time to speak,
> a time to love and a time to hate,
> a time for war and a time for peace.

I love the words "a season for every activity." I find this phrase comforting and confronting at the same time. It's comforting when I feel impatient about wanting to accomplish something in the future—knowing the time will come, the season will be ripe for harvest of whatever that desire is. The verse is confronting because it cautions me to be careful, to go slowly, not to plant seeds in the dead of winter. Which season are you in right now? Look at your entire life—your age, the age of your spouse and children, your job, your finances, your church commitments, even where you live. Does one of these verses particularly strike your heart in a given area?

If you feel convicted to make changes in your life, do it slowly. Any change you make will always affect those around you. If you feel the Lord calling you out of a situation, who will be affected? You, your family, your friends, co-workers, or relatives? No decision to act is ever unilateral. If you do feel led to drop certain activities to be able to invest yourself in stillness, be sure not to refill those empty spots of time with some other activity. I think we sometimes fool ourselves into thinking that when we drop something, we have twice as much time as we did before and we fill that slot with three things!

Make a one-month, a six-month, and a twelve-month plan for yourself about how you will turn your attention to the Lord. As part of the plan, write out specific goals for how you will decrease spiritual attention deficit in your life. Consider what things, thoughts, and actions tend to take your focus off the Lord. Write out in your journal your promises to yourself for how you will remember stillness in the midst of chaos. Will you turn back to your notes from reading this book? Will you recite Scripture you've memorized? Will you review the "Stillness in Action" points?

A written plan will act to reassure you, inspire you, motivate you, and convict you all at once. When a promise or plan is written in ink, it moves your thoughts from mere conjecture to reality.

I have a strong conviction that God wants you to draw closer to Him, to be in deep fellowship and communion with Him. I know He wants your undivided attention. I wish I could talk with each woman who reads this book to hear just how He will draw you in, how you will respond, how He'll equip you, and the wonderful relationship you will grow with Him. Each of your stories will be different, but you *will* each have a story of how adopting a still lifestyle has changed your relationship with God.

Stillness in Action

Plan a day or an overnight retreat. Even if you have to schedule it many weeks ahead, block out the time on your calendar, make arrangements for your house and children, and GO! Visit someplace that will offer you quiet and rest. A lake cottage, an oceanfront hotel, a country bed-and-breakfast. Go someplace where there aren't distracting phones, television, or activities.

Even if your personality thrives on lots of activity, make a commitment to being entirely alone. Pray for God to prepare your heart for this time with Him, and pray that He will meet you at your designated "holy place." Use this time to write out your personal plan of action for embracing a still life.

MEMORY VERSE

"I do not concern myself with great matters or things too wonderful for me. But I have stilled and quieted my soul."

PSALM 131:1–2

Notes

Preface

1. Charles R. Swindoll, *Intimacy With the Almighty* (Dallas, Tex.: Word Publishing, Inc., 1996), 62.

Chapter Two

1. M. Beth Cutaiar, *Just for Girls* (Wheaton, Ill.: Crossway Books, 1999).

Chapter Three

1. Jane Kise, David Stark, and Sandra Krebs Hirsh, *LifeKeys* (Minneapolis: Bethany House Publishers, 1996); Jane Kise and David Stark, *LifeDirections* (Minneapolis: Bethany House Publishers, 1999); Betty Southard and Marita Littauer, *Come As You Are* (Minneapolis: Bethany House Publishers, 1999); and for youth, Jane Kise and Kevin Johnson, *Find Your Fit* (Minneapolis: Bethany House Publishers, 1998).

2. Pam Farrel, *Woman of Influence* (Downers Grove, Ill.: InterVarsity Press, 1996), 58.

Chapter Four

1. Phillip Keller, *A Shepherd Looks at Psalm 23* (Grand Rapids, Mich.: Zondervan, 1970), 35.

2. Emilie Griffin, *Wilderness Time: A Guide for Spiritual Retreat*

(New York: HarperCollins, 1997), 23.

3. Swindoll, 36.

Chapter Five

1. Swindoll, 73.

Chapter Six

1. Tony Evans, *Our God Is Awesome* (Chicago, Ill.: Moody Press, 1994), 28.

Chapter Seven

1. G. I. Williamson, *The Shorter Catechism* (Phillipsburg, N.J.: Presbyterian and Reformed Publishing Co., 1970), 5.

Chapter Eight

1. Griffin, 35.

Chapter Nine

1. Evans, 22.

Chapter Ten

1. Ibid., 46.

2. Kay Arthur, *To Know Him by Name* (Sisters, Ore.: Multnomah Books, 1995), 9.

3. From Integrity's *Hosanna!* 1993. Used with permission.

Chapter Eleven

1. Evans, 74.

Chapter Twelve

1. Farrel, 67.

2. Swindoll, 73.

3. Evans, 46.